Niaz Ahmed

ISBN: 1-58112-084-2

DISSERTATION.COM

2000

ISBN: 1-58112-084-2

Dissertation.com
USA – 2000

www.dissertation.com/library/1120842a.htm

University of Southern Mississippi

CROSS-CULTURAL CONTENT ANALYSIS OF ADVERTISING

FROM THE UNITED STATES AND INDIA

by

Niaz Ahmed

Abstract of a Dissertation
Submitted to the Graduate School
of the University of Southern Mississippi
in Partial Fulfillment of the Requirements
for the Degree of Doctor of Philosophy

May 1996

ABSTRACT

CROSS-CULTURAL CONTENT ANALYSIS OF ADVERTISING

FROM THE UNITED STATES AND INDIA

by

Niaz Ahmed

May 1996

This cross-cultural content analysis (which merged traditional content analysis method with semiotic concepts) compared advertising in the United States (a highly individualistic and low-context culture) and India (a highly collectivist and high-context culture). The study examined the characteristics, differences and similarities in advertising strategies and expressions. A stratified random sample of advertisements for consumer products was selected from nationally circulated news magazines and business magazines of each country between January 1993 and December 1994 (*Time* and *Business Week* from the United States; *India Today* and *Business India* from India).

This study found that there were significant differences in the way the two cultures produced advertising messages and that differential cultural values were reflected in their advertising expressions. The findings revealed that the U.S. advertisements utilized direct rhetorical styles, individualistic visual stances, sexual portrayals of women and comparative approaches more often than their Indian counterparts. The Indian ads utilized indirect rhetorical styles, collective visual stances and stereotypical portrayals of women more frequently than did the U.S. ads.

The evidence of specific cross-cultural differences suggests that perhaps the proponents of "standardization of international advertising" have promoted an oversimplification. This cross-cultural study suggests that caution should be exercised when considering standardization in advertising and other forms of promotional communication between divergent cultures.

iv

University of Southern Mississippi

CROSS-CULTURAL CONTENT ANALYSIS OF ADVERTISING

FROM THE UNITED STATES AND INDIA

by

Niaz Ahmed

A Dissertation
Submitted to the Graduate School
of the University of Southern Mississippi
in Partial Fulfillment of the Requirements
for the Degree of Doctor of Philosophy

Approved:

_____
Director

_____

_____

_____

_____

_____
Dean of the Graduate School

May 1996

vi

DEDICATION

TO MY

PARENTS

ACKNOWLEDGMENTS

The author wishes to express sincere gratitude to Professor Mazharul Haque for his guidance during all phases of this research. In addition special thanks are due to Drs. David Goff, Gene Wiggins, Arthur Kaul and William Schoell for their assistance. The author is especially grateful to his parents and Zinia for their personal support and inspiration.

TABLE OF CONTENTS

CHAPTER I

INTRODUCTION

The phenomenon of advertising has long been a subject of research in several disciplines such as mass communication, marketing, sociology, cultural anthropology, social psychology, semiotics and cultural studies. One area that has attracted a great deal of attention in several disciplines during the last two decades is the analysis of mass media advertising content to gain insights into how cultural factors affect advertising strategies and expressions; how cultural values, norms and stereotypes are reflected in advertising; how advertising creates meanings and affects the audience and the larger society over time (e.g., Berman, 1981; Eco, 1977, 1979; Haskins & Kendrick, 1991; Leiss, Kline & Jhally, 1986; McQuail, 1994; Noth, 1990; Vestergaard & Schroder, 1985; Williamson, 1978). Whether from a quantitative, qualitative or interpretative perspective, whether a researcher follows the modern social scientific approach, critical theory perspective or postmodernist approach, analysis of advertising and other media content is of growing importance.

Although the phenomenon of advertising has been studied for several decades, cross-cultural advertising research is a relatively new area of study. In recent years, the study of cross-cultural advertising has become a subject of increasing importance because of several important developments:

• As the integration of the world economy has increased significantly in recent years and as nations of the world have become increasingly economically interdependent through international trade--diverse people and cultures are coming into contact through interpersonal interaction as well as advertising and other media images and messages. In an increasingly global economic environment, international trade has achieved phenomenal growth resulting in increased international mass media advertising across diverse cultures (Mooij & Keegan, 1991).

• Recent developments in several regions of the world--such as the disintegration of the Soviet Union and its adoption of free enterprise systems, democratization of the Eastern Europe and its transformation to a market economy, reunification of Germany, the formation of the EU, export-led rapid economic growth of the NICs (Newly Industrialized Countries), and opening of markets in Asia and Latin America--have revitalized the notion of a global marketplace, and encouraged many marketers to internationalize their businesses.

11

• The marketing debates about globalization of markets came to the forefront in the 1980s and continue today to polarize advertising practitioners and researchers over the question of whether or not consumers around the world are becoming homogeneous (in terms of values, desires and tastes) (Cateora, 1987; Hite & Fraser, 1988; Levitt, 1983; Onkvisit & Shaw, 1985).

• The "cultural imperialism" issue has attracted a great deal of attention over the impact of Western advertising and other media products on the cultures of developing nations (Fejes, 1980; Mattelart, 1983; Schiller, 1983).

• In recent years, there has been an increasing interest over the issue of how advertising reflects, reinforces and affects cultural values of its target audience (Holbrook, 1987; Pollay, 1986, 1987).

Cross-cultural analysis of advertising can identify specific differences and similarities in advertising strategies, expressions, and manifest cultural values, norms and stereotypes of the target audience and the larger culture. Such findings may be used to address the question of whether the same strategies and expressions can be used in international advertising, and whether the values, attitudes, desires and tastes of consumers around the world are converging (e.g., Frith & Wesson, 1991; Hong, Muderrrisoglu & Zinkhan, 1987; Mueller, 1987).

Comparative analysis of advertising from Western industrialized countries and Eastern developing countries may reveal specific similarities or differences in manifest cultural values, norms and stereotypes in line with, or divergent from, those of Western nations. Such information can be used to address the question of cultural imperialism and the debates over whether and how advertising reflects, reinforces and affects cultural values of its target audience. On the other hand, findings about gender role portrayals in advertising may reveal how sex roles are changing in these societies, and to what extent the images of the sexes in advertising are keeping pace with social change.

From a more pragmatic standpoint, if specific cross-cultural differences or similarities in advertising strategies, expressions and manifest values and norms can be identified, researchers and practitioners will better understand which aspects of advertising can be shared across several countries, and conversely, which aspects need to be adapted to local cultures. As indicated by previous research, many advertising strategies and expressions (e.g., direct or indirect comparative technique; rational or emotional approach; individualistic stance or collective stance in visuals; direct or indirect rhetorical styles; high or low level of information cues, emphasis on certain information cues) may be influenced by important cultural values such as individualism, collectivism, rational reasoning, emotionalism, and low context culture vs. high context culture (e.g., Cutler & Javalgi, 1992; Frith & Wesson, 1991; Hong, Muderrisoglu & Zinkhan, 1987).

From the standpoint of international marketing and advertising practitioners, such cross-cultural understanding is imperative in order to be able to formulate effective localized advertising that would appeal to or reflect the cultural values and norms of its intended audience (Belk & Pollay, 1985; Munson & McIntyre, 1979; Henry, 1976). In a broader sense, a localized approach is beneficial not only to the international marketer (more effective in getting its message across) but also to the larger host society (its culture is not adversely affected by alien values, beliefs and lifestyles).

Although several cross-cultural content analyses of advertising have been conducted in recent years, most of them compared either two or more Western industrialized countries or two or more Western and Eastern industrialized countries (only two studies included a developing country). For example, Weinberger and Spotts (1989) comparatively analyzed the information content of British and U.S. television advertising; Biswas, Olsen and Carlet (1992) conducted a comparative content analysis of information content and emotional appeals in print advertisements from the United States and France; Cutler and Javalgi (1992) conducted a cross-cultural analysis of the visual components of print advertising from the United States, France and the United Kingdom; Frith and Wesson (1991) conducted a comparative content analysis to examine manifest cultural values in advertising of the United States and England; Ramaprasad (1992) comparatively analyzed the information content of American and Japanese television commercials; Mueller (1987), examined the usage of advertising appeals in magazine advertisements of the United States and Japan; Madden, Caballero and Masukubo (1986) analyzed the information content in Japanese and U.S. magazine advertising; Hong et al. (1987) also examined the information content of U.S. and Japanese magazine advertising.

13

The only two cross-cultural studies involving developed and developing countries were Gilly's (1988) study comparing gender portrayals in advertising of the United States, Australia and Mexico, and Alden, Hoyer & Lee's (1993) study examining the use of humor in advertising of the United States, Germany, Thailand and South Korea. To date, there is no cross-cultural study that comparatively analyzes advertising in India and the United States.

Evidently, there is a need for cross-cultural advertising studies about industrially developing countries in the Eastern cultural environment and highly industrialized countries in the Western cultural context. Moreover, there is a need for more comprehensive cross-cultural approaches to the analysis and interpretation of the verbal as well as visual content of advertising. Most previous cross-cultural advertising studies were conducted following the traditional quantitative content analysis method and examined only the verbal content of advertising. One reason for this narrow approach is that the traditional quantitative content analysis method is not very effective in analyzing culture-specific elements and connotations in visual content of advertising. In single-country analysis (e.g. U.S. advertising), some qualitative researchers have used semiotics and other interpretative methods to analyze the linguistic as well as visual content of advertising (e.g., Barthes, 1964, 1977; Eco, 1977, 1979; Vestergaard & Schroder, 1985; Williamson, 1978). However, in cross-cultural advertising studies, analysis of the verbal content has been the most dominant direction. Whether from a pragmatic perspective (e.g. international marketing and advertising), or critical perspective (e.g., cultural studies), analysis of only the verbal content is not sufficient to address the important issues of cross-cultural advertising. This is due to advertising's generally communicating its messages not only through its verbal content but also in conjunction with its visual content.

With this realization in recent years, a few well-known researchers in several disciplines (e.g., marketing, sociology, anthropology) combined the traditional quantitative content analysis method with semiotic concepts and approaches to study advertising communication (e.g., Frith & Wesson, 1991; Leiss, Kline & Jhally, 1986; Umiker-Sebeok, 1987). This new interdisciplinary approach has been gaining importance since the First International Conference on Semiotics and

14

Marketing in 1985 and the establishment of a new publication entitled Marketing Signs . This new approach can be extended to a cross-cultural study of advertising to examine both verbal and visual content. Indeed, the merging of semiotic concepts and traditional quantitative content analysis is extremely useful in cross-cultural analysis because semiotic concepts can be effectively applied in examining visual content of advertising.

In this context, a cross-cultural analysis of the verbal as well as visual content of print advertising in India and the United States was conducted to examine the characteristics, differences and similarities in advertising strategies and expressions. The study followed the traditional content analysis method. However, following the new interdisciplinary approach, some semiotic concepts were applied as well.

The advertising was analyzed and compared in terms of

1. Linguistic codification (informational, directive, poetic and expressive peech acts).

2. Visual codification (iconic stance of characters, indexical value transfer, iconic image of women).

3. Combined verbal/visual codification (direct and indirect comparative approach).

The results of this study are expected to provide cross-cultural understanding and insights into the nature of advertising in the 1990s in the United States and India. The comparative and descriptive analyses are expected to offer an in-depth understanding of the characteristics, similarities and differences in advertising strategies and expressions of India and the United States. This study is also the first to provide a comprehensive cross-cultural approach to the analysis and interpretation of the verbal as well as visual content of advertising. The results will be of particular interest to those international marketers entering the markets of India and the United States and other countries with similar cultures and socioeconomic environments.

This study will also be used as a basis for a future study that will examine the comparative effectiveness as well as social-cultural effects of various types of advertising

15

expressions on the audiences of India and the United States. The current study can be viewed as in the tradition of the "cultivation analysis" method which analyzes and documents dominant messages and themes in media content, and then, through a separate study of the audience, examines the effects of such messages on the heavy media users (Wimmer & Dominick, 1991). A similar method was also used by Stewart and Furse (1986) to examine content characteristics and effectiveness of advertising in the United States. Stewart and Furse conducted a content analysis of U.S. television commercials, and later through a separate experimental study examined which advertising strategies and expressions resulted in greater commercial effectiveness.

CHAPTER II

LITERATURE REVIEW

Most of the cross-cultural empirical studies that have been conducted to date compared either two or more Western industrialized countries or Western and Eastern industrial countries (with a few exceptions). Studies that conducted cross-cultural content analysis and provide background information for conceptual analysis will be reviewed first. Other related studies that do not fall under the umbrella of cross-cultural content analysis but are relevant and useful in understanding the issues of cross-cultural advertising will also be reviewed.

Cross-Cultural Content Analysis of Advertising

Weinberger and Spotts (1989) conducted a comparative content analysis of the information content in television advertising in the United States and the United Kingdom. The results revealed that U.S. television advertising contained a higher level of information content than British advertising. A comparison between the U.S. sample and a 1977 Resnik and Stern study showed that informativeness has increased in U.S. advertising over a decade. Overall, the ads for high involvement and rational products contained higher information content. The researchers concluded that the differences between the U.S. and British advertising are related to the underlying sociocultural setting in the respective countries.

Biswas, Olsen and Carlet (1992) comparatively analyzed magazine advertisements of France and the United States in terms of information content, emotional appeals, use of humor and sex. The study revealed that French advertisements made greater use of emotional appeals, humor and sex appeals, while U.S. advertisements contained a greater number of information cues.

Cutler and Javalgi (1992) conducted a comparative analysis of the visual content of print advertising from the United States, France and England. The results revealed greater country differences than similarities in terms of various visual components in advertising. Differences were found in seven elements (size of the visual, use of black & white visuals, use of photograph

17

as opposed to illustrations, size of product in the visual, product comparison, use of symbolic process appeal, frequency of portraying children in the visual). Similarities were found in product portrayal, minority portrayal and elderly portrayal. The researchers suggested that international advertisers should standardize or localize visual elements of their advertising accordingly.

Frith and Wesson (1991) compared the content of print advertising from the United States and England in terms of manifest cultural values. The study found that magazine advertisements in the United States portrayed characters in more "individualistic" stances than British advertisements. On the other hand, British advertisements made social class differences more evident. Based on the findings, the researchers suggested that because of cultural differences uniform international advertising will not be effective.

Belk and Bryce (1986) examined television advertisements in Japan and the United States. Using a content analysis method they attempted to determine if there was any cultural value difference in advertising in terms of materialism and individual determinism. The study found that the U.S. advertisements placed more emphasis on individual determinism and materialism.

Mueller (1987) examined magazine advertisements of Japan and the United States. Using a content analysis method, the author compared the themes in advertising and concluded that there were considerable similarities among the consumers in the two countries. The researcher found that the same basic advertising appeals were used in both U.S. and Japanese advertisements. However, the degree to which these appeals were used varied from one country to another. Muller suggests that the sensitivity to cultural differences is reflected through the varied degrees of the same appeals. The author concluded that appeals such as product merit and status appeal are universal.

Hong et al. (1987) comparatively analyzed magazine advertisements of Japan and the United States to determine how advertising expressions and content differed in the two cultures. The variables examined were emotional appeals, informativeness and comparativeness of

18

advertising. The analysis revealed that Japanese advertisements were more emotional and less comparative than the U.S. advertisements. In terms of information content, there was no difference in the advertisements of the two countries.

Tansey, Hyman and Zinkhan (1990) conducted a content analysis of Brazilian and U.S. auto advertisements to determine the extent of work themes, urban themes and leisure themes. The analysis of automobile advertisements in business magazines of Brazil and the United Statesrevealed that urban themes were used more frequently in Brazilian advertisements than in the U.S. advertisements, while leisure themes were used more frequently in the U.S. advertisements. The extent of work themes was found to be similar in Brazilian and U.S. advertising. The researchers concluded that cultural values differ between the business classes of the United States and Brazil. The authors noted that these findings provide evidence against use of similar themes across cultures.

Gilly (1988) compared sex role portrayals in television advertisements of the United States, Australia and Mexico. Results of this comparative content analysis revealed that sex role stereotypes are present in advertising in all three countries, but are manifested in different ways. Among the three countries, the Australian advertising displayed fewer sex role differences than the U.S. and Mexican advertising. Comparing the findings about Australian advertising with the studies conducted 12 years ago, the researcher found that sex role portrayals have changed over the years (less stereotypical now). The researcher noted that international marketers should be aware of the cultural norms in terms of sex role portrayals as well as how they are changing.

Ramaprasad and Hasegawa (1992) compared the information content of television commercials in Japan and the United States. The findings revealed that most Japanese and U.S. commercials emphasized similar kinds of information cues. However, they differed in the average number of cues employed in some product and strategy categories. The authors suggested caution in using the same advertising approaches in the United States and Japan.

Rice and Lu (1988) conducted a content analysis of Chinese magazine advertisements. The researchers analyzed the levels of advertising information based on type of magazine and type of product. The findings indicated that Chinese magazine advertisements contained relatively large amounts of information compared to previous content analyses of Western advertising.

Alden, Hoyer and Lee (1993) conducted a cross-cultural analysis of the use of humor in advertising. The researchers examined the content of humorous television advertising from Korea, Germany, Thailand and the United States. Their findings revealed that humorous advertising in these diverse cultures shares certain universal cognitive structures underlying the message. However, the results indicated that the specific content of humorous advertising was likely to vary along major normative dimensions such as individualism and collectivism.

Klassen, Jasper and Schartz (1993) examined how men and women are portrayed in magazine advertisements in the United States. A longitudinal content analysis of United States magazine advertisements revealed that a disproportionately high number of advertisements portrayed women in traditional poses relative to advertisements that featured men and women together as equals. However, the traditional portrayals of women have been decreasing since the early 1980s, and "equality portrayals" are increasing.

Other Relevant and Related Studies

Britt (1974) identified and discussed three factors that might affect the transferability of advertising: consumption patterns, psychological characteristics and cultural criteria. The author suggested that if pattern of purchase and usage varies widely in the target countries then direct transfer of advertising would not be effective. Britt also argues that if the consumers in the target countries have very similar psychological characteristics, such as the same motivation for purchase or favorable attitude toward the brand name, then the same strategy could be used. If the characteristics vary from country to country, then the same advertising appeal would not work. Finally the author suggests that cultural factors, such as social stigma or tradition, may have a significant impact on the way the product and its advertising message would be perceived by the consumers of that culture.

Dunn (1976) conducted a survey of U.S. multinational managers to determine the relative importance of various factors affecting transferability of advertising. The researcher found that the majority of the multinational managers who responded to the questionnaires ranked "rate of economic growth of country" to be the most important variable in making advertising transfer decisions. Other factors that were perceived to be important were the following: eating patterns and customs, average size of household, social class structure, attitudes toward authority, degree of nationalism in country, attitudes toward achievement and work, attitudes toward risk taking, attitudes toward wealth and monetary gain, similarity of ethical and moral standard to the United States.

Twelve years later, Hite and Fraser (1988) conducted a similar survey of U.S. multinational managers and found that "rate of economic growth" is still an important factor that affects the transferability of advertising. Other related factors that were perceived to be important include brand name acceptance, education level, government control of media, nationalism, attitudes of people toward the United States and eating patterns of people. These factors were adopted from Dunn's (1976) list of 31 factors. A comparison of this study with that of Dunn's indicates that some of the factors gained more importance over the years.

Cundiff and Hilger (1984) conducted a survey that found the following factors to be important: levels of economic development, consumption pattern, cultural diversity, and brand name acceptance. An international marketer must analyze each market before formulating an international advertising strategy. The authors also indicated that cultural diversity and translation problems discourage standardization of advertising message. The authors identified some cultural factors such as individualism vs. conformity, conservatism vs. desire for change, social mobility vs. social stability, and suspicion vs. credibility. It is suggested that such cultural factors have a significant impact on consumers' perceptions of international advertising messages. The researchers also indicate that if the consumers in the target countries use the product in similar ways, if it satisfies the same needs and if the buyer motivation is the same, then the same strategies or tactics can be effectively used in all target countries.

21

Ricks, Arpan and Fu (1974) discussed several factors that could have a significant impact on international advertising. The authors reported several cases of international advertising failure and showed how linguistic and cultural factors influenced the consumers' perception of international advertising. The authors suggest that different languages, customs, attitudes, preferences and needs make it necessary to adapt to local conditions. The researchers indicated that most international advertising blunders occur because the advertisers fail to understand and consider cultural differences. The researchers recommended the effective use of local experts in the planning and implementation of international advertising campaigns.

The Green and Langeard (1975) study attempted to determine if there were differences in characteristics and behaviors between U.S. and French consumers (innovators). The researchers utilized a sample of 193 Texan women and 226 French women. Based on responses to mailed and self-administered questionnaires, the researchers found that there were significant differences in media use and buying habits for tangible products and services.

Boote (1983) investigated the psychographic characteristics of consumers in the United Kingdom, Germany and France. A 29-item value scale was employed to measure a random sample of women in each of these countries. The results revealed that there were some similarities within subgroups of the three countries. However, there were some differences as well. The consumers of the three countries ranked the value statements differently.

Caffyn and Rogers (1970) attempted to determine if British consumers would perceive British and U.S. television advertisements differently. The researchers surveyed 1,200 British consumers and found significant differences in the perception of British and U.S. commercials. The results indicated that the British consumers perceived the U.S. ads to be entertaining but less persuasive than the British ads. The researchers suggested that sociocultural and marketing differences between the United Kingdom and the United States might render a standardized approach ineffective.

Colvin, Heeler and Thorpe (1980) examined the applicability of a combination strategy or the so-called pattern standardization. The researchers utilized stratified samples of British,

French and German car buyers. Respondents were asked to rank 27 automobile attributes and purchase interest. The findings revealed that a single-theme strategy could be used in some countries, while modifications were required for other countries.

An earlier study by Donnelly (1970) examined the relationship between an advertising manager's attitude toward the importance of cultural variables and the international advertising strategy employed by his or her firm. Based on a sample of 121 U.S. advertising managers, the findings revealed a significant relationship between the variable of attitude toward culture and strategy employed. The results indicated that the companies in which the advertising managers believed cultural differences were important utilized more decentralized planning and localized message.

The literature reviewed clearly indicates that almost all (with two exceptions) cross-cultural content analysis of advertising has concerned only industrially developed countries. The surveys that were conducted in related areas were also mostly about industrially developed countries. Needless to say, there is a great need for comparative analysis of advertising from developing and developed countries.

CHAPTER III

CONCEPTUAL ANALYSIS

This section discusses several concepts and theories which will provide a conceptual background for the present cross-cultural study.

Communication and Culture

The influence of culture on communication is well documented by researchers in many disciplines. One of the most difficult challenges for international marketers is communicating to people of diverse cultures. Cultural differences may exist not only between nations but also within a nation itself. Such cultural and microcultural differences present a formidable challenge to international marketing and advertising practitioners because the value systems, attitudes, perceptions and communication of individuals and groups are all culturally shaped or influenced (Samover & Porter, 1991; Tan, 1986).

As research indicates, advertising, a form of social communication, is also influenced by various elements of the originating culture (e.g., Frith & Wesson, 1991; Hong et al., 1987; Mueller, 1987; Rice & Lu, 1988; Tansey et al., 1990). On the other hand, cultural values may determine the differential meanings that people derive from advertising messages (Cundiff & Hilger, 1984; Hornik, 1980; McCracken, 1986; Onkvisit & Shaw, 1983). Advertising may also shape or affect the values of its consumers over time (Ewen & Ewen, 1982; Ferguson et al., 1990; Pollay, 1986, 1987).

In his research reports, Pollay stated that advertising was a "distorted mirror" in that it reflects only certain underlying values and lifestyles. He also noted that advertising was a "distorting mirror" as well, because it strengthened those values by providing reinforcement, and these reinforced and strengthened values then would feedback into the culture. "Cultural evolution can be expected toward the values seen in commercial communication" (Pollay, 1987, p. 108).

24

It is well documented in many disciplines (e.g., sociology, cultural anthropology, mass communication, marketing, cultural studies, semiotics) that advertising reflects and reinforces many of the social values, norms and stereotypes of its audiences (Coser et al., 1987; Holbrook, 1987; McQuail, 1994; Mueller, 1987; Vestergaard & Schroder, 1985). Two well-known semiotic researchers, Fiske and Hartley (1978, 1980) noted that advertising does not represent the "manifest actuality" of the society, but rather symbolically reflects the social values. The researchers pointed out that advertising insists on an idealized goal of achieving personal happiness, success and security, and it does this by first depicting a world--overrepresented by young, beautiful, successful, happy, wealthy people, and then creating a desire in the audience to better their lives or to achieve the desirable attributes of the people in the advertisement, and finally it portrays the product (explicitly, implicitly or symbolically) as a bridge toward achieving that goal (Vesterguaard & Schroder, 1985). However, in order to attract and hold the attention of the potential consumers and create a favorable attitude toward the product, advertising must reflect the cultural values and norms of the society. Therefore, it is possible to gain an insight into the current social values and norms (values may change over time) by analyzing the structures of meaning found in advertisements. Analysis of advertising and other media content is preferred by many quantitative as well as qualitative researchers over surveys of the audience, because people are not always able to identify the cultural values, norms, beliefs and attitudes which they take for granted (Frith & Wesson, 1991; Noth, 1990; Vestergaard & Schroder, 1985).

In the still-new area of cross-cultural advertising research, a few researchers have used analysis of advertising content not only to gain insights into cross-cultural differences and similarities in advertising strategies and expressions, but also to understand what cultural values, norms and stereotypes are manifested in various advertising strategies and expressions across several countries. Since cross-cultural analysis of advertising is a new research area, many of the previous researchers developed their conceptual framework by borrowing concepts and

25

theories from disciplines such as sociology, cultural anthropology, social psychology and cultural studies.

Advertising and Semiotics

An examination of the existing semiotic methods indicates that various schools of semiotics have developed quite different approaches to the study of advertising, and yet there are common aspects in these approaches: the extension of analysis from the verbal to the visual and the non-verbal messages is a central focus in all semiotic analysis of advertising (Noth, 1990).

Barthes (1964, 1977) identified three kinds of elements in an illustrated advertisement: linguistic message, uncoded iconic message (visual) and coded iconic or symbolic message (visual). The linguistic message relies on the code of language. The uncoded iconic message consists of the photographic image which analogously represents the "real" objects. The symbolic message includes the connotations of the picture and the verbal message which form the "image" of the product.

Eco (1977, 79) divided advertising codes into verbal codification and visual codification. He identified several levels of visual codification including the iconic level, which is similar to the uncoded iconic message in Barthes's typology, and the iconographic level, which is based on cultural and historical traditions and genre conventions.

Pierce's original typology of signs (icon, index, symbol) has also been applied by several semiotic researchers to the study of visual content of advertising (e.g., Noth, 1988; Vestergaard & Schroder, 1985). According to Vestergaard & Schroder's (1985) analysis, there are three types of relations between a sign and its object (what it represents). Iconic signs communicate through resemblance or similarity, and the relation between sign and object is natural or motivated. For example, the drawing or photographic image of a product or person represents or denotes the real object. The similarity may also be established through convention, such as a circle encompassing three lines and a curve may represent a smiling or a sad face depending on whether the curve turns upwards or downwards. The simplest form of advertising illustration is a picture of the

26

product against a neutral background. Iconic relation may also be found in the use of language. For example, in a metaphorical expression, two words have iconic relations in the sense that one word is replaced by another word which is similar to it in meaning, or the meaning has been established by convention. An example of the metaphorical use of language in advertising is Exxon's (in Europe Esso) famous slogan: "put a tiger in your tank," in which the word "tiger" is metaphorically used in place of "strength."

An indexical sign can be used to represent its object because it usually occurs in close association with it. In language, an example of this is the use of the word "crown" for "king." In the area of visuals, indexical images are often used in advertising. Advertising illustrations often try to establish an indexical relation between the product and some desirable attributes of a person or situation. This process is also referred to as indexical feature transfer, or indexical value transfer (Noth, 1990). Since it is often impossible to show the special features or use value of the product iconically (or because it does not have any differentiating features), the product is associated with persons, objects or situations whose desirable attributes are well known. For example, a diamond ring advertisement associates the "diamond ring" with "love" by showing an enlarged picture of the ring with a picture of a young couple. Thus a visual metaphor is used to create an indexical relation: diamond ring=love. Johnnie Walker Scotch Whisky advertising often creates an indexical relation by showing the product being used by rich people who live in mansions and drive expensive cars and it is suggested that they have "good taste." The advertising associates wealth and elegance with sophistication and quality, and this attribute is then transferred to the product. Thus Scotch Whisky becomes associated with high-class people and upscale living. Again, a visual metaphor is used to create an indexical relation: Scotch Whisky = sophistication and elegance=high-class, upscale living.

Symbolic signs communicate by cultural convention and traditions. Examples of culture-specific symbols include the following: the cross symbolizes Christian faith; the dove symbolizes hope and peace, a meaning derived from the biblical story about the returning of the dove to Noah's ark with an olive branch, indicating that the water was receding; the snake symbolizes deception in the West because of its cultural meaning derived from the Old Testament (in some Asian cultures the snake is a symbol of rebirth and immortality because it sheds its skins and becomes "new" again); the color white symbolizes death in some cultures, while the color black is a symbol of death in many cultures; an image of the heart symbolizes love in many cultures. In product packaging and advertising, arbitrary symbols are sometimes used to establish a link between the image and the product (e.g., the symbols of Mercedes Benz, Coca-Cola, Dodge).

Linguistic Codification of Advertising

According to linguistics and semiotics, in communication, language can perform several functions or speech acts (Searle, 1971, 1969; Vestergaard & Schroder, 1985). In the expressive function or expressive speech act, language focuses on the addresser, his or her feelings, attitudes, wishes. In advertising, expressive speech act occurs when the advertiser/company, for example, identifies and praises itself and recommends its product (e.g. "another fine product from Procter & Gamble"), condemns or criticizes its competitors, apologizes for inconvenience caused by faulty parts and the like. In the directive function or directive speech act, language relates to the addressee, and tries to influence the addressee's beliefs, attitudes, emotions and actions. In advertising, directive speech act is often used to call upon the audience to act (directly or indirectly). For example, the targeted consumers are asked to try the product, or get the product, use the product, choose the brand ("buy" is generally not used because of its unpleasant connotations), to "return" to the product and the like. Sometimes more indirect ways of calling to action are used (e.g., "Isn't it time you introduced your family to brand X?" or "why not change to X?"). In the informational function or information speech act, language is oriented towards straight, logical facts and information. In advertising, informational speech act is used to describe or inform about the product attributes and features. The poetic function or poetic speech act takes place when the linguistic code is used in a special way to communicate a certain meaning, double meaning or ambiguity. Some poetic devices used in advertising include verbal metaphor, simile and rhyme.

28

The linguistic content of advertising can be classified according to this typology of "speech act" or "function of language." Advertising in diverse cultures may differ in terms of these speech acts. There may be differential emphasis on different speech acts or functions of language depending on different characteristics of diverse cultures. The following review of the previous studies will illustrate and discuss these concepts.

High-Context vs. Low-Context Culture, Purpose of Communication and Differential Speech Acts in Advertising

Cultural characteristics (such as low context vs. high context culture, views about the purpose of communication) may be reflected in the way different cultures emphasize different types of information cues or rhetorical devices.

A high-context culture is one in which the context, suggestive or connotative meanings of the message, may be more important than the words themselves (Cundiff & Hilger, 1984; Hall, 1976). In a high-context culture, the audience is likely to derive meaning from the context, reducing the need for explicit verbal messages. A low-context culture is one where explicit verbal messages are direct. In order to communicate effectively, messages must be explicitly and directly stated through words containing most of the information to be sent. For example, France is a comparatively higher context culture than the United States; Americans are direct and pay more attention to details (Cateora, 1983). The French allow their imagination and intuition to make up for the implied meanings, and are more interested in the general effect from an aesthetic perspective. The distinct differences between communication styles of the British and Americans have also been noted. While Americans are characterized by directness in speech, indirectness characterizes interpersonal as well as institutional communication in England, where a considerable emphasis is placed on double meanings, ambiguities and plays on words (Burli-Storz, 1980; Leech, 1966; Rothenberg, 1989).

Within the Eastern cultural environment, Japan is known to be a high- context culture. The Japanese language is very sensitive and emotive and not very directed toward logical

29

exactness; it places more emphasis on referring to emotional and aesthetic statuses of mind. Indirectness, subtlety and symbolism are important characteristics of the Japanese culture (Hong et al., 1987). Different cultures may also differ on their views about the purpose of communication. For example, Americans supposedly place more emphasis on the persuasive purpose-- communication as a means of persuading others, influencing attitudes or behavior. In contrast, Europeans place less emphasis on the persuasive function of communication, and place more emphasis on the view of communication as a process through which shared culture is created, modified and transmitted (Carey, 1973).

Such cultural differences may be reflected in advertising strategies and expressions as suggested by several researchers. For example, compared to U.S. advertising, French and British advertisements contain more emotional appeals and utilize more indirect and poetic rhetorical devices (poetic speech act), such as metaphors, similes, double meanings and philosophic and euphemistic expressions (Biswas et al., 1992; Cutler & Javalgi, 1992; Hall & Hall, 1990). The U.S. advertising directly, clearly and logically presents information, facts and evidence about product merits and purchase reasons (informational speech act), contains more informational cues than French and British advertising (Biswas et al., 1992; Hong et al., 1987; Weinberger & Spotts, 1989), and utilizes direct rhetorical devices such as an imperative (directive speech act) (Frith & Wesson, 1991). Within an Eastern cultural context, Japanese advertising uses emotional or "soft-sell" approach more frequently than rational or "hard-sell" approach as compared to U.S. advertising (Hong et al., 1987; Mueller, 1987).

Cultural differences may also be reflected in the ways different countries emphasize different types of information cues in their advertising, because consumers may value various attributes differently. For example, Japanese magazine advertising emphasizes price information, while magazine advertisements in the United States use this information cue less often (Hong et al., 1987). Compared to U.S. magazine advertisements, Japanese advertising also places greater emphasis on information about safety features and product packaging (Madden et

30

al., 1986). An analysis of Chinese magazine advertising (single-country analysis) revealed that information about product performance and quality was emphasized (Rice & Lu, 1988). Such findings are useful because several surveys indicated that consumers in different cultures value various attributes differently (e.g., Colvin et al., 1980; Green et al., 1975).

From the perspective of international marketing and advertising practitioners, it is useful to understand how a particular culture expresses its advertising messages in terms of linguistic content; what type of speech act it emphasizes (e.g., informational, directive, poetic, expressive); whether it values a high level of information cues or informational speech acts in its advertising; and what types of information cues it emphasizes. The implications are that emphasizing the wrong approach in international advertising would lead to a serious communication failure or ineffectiveness.

Visual Codification of Advertising

In addition to low-context vs. high-context cultural traits, other characteristics such as power distance, and individualistic vs. collectivist culture, may also be reflected in the way advertisements codify the visual elements.

Individualistic vs. Collectivist Culture and Iconic Stance of Characters

It is well documented that cultures vary in terms of degree of individualism and collectivism. Western cultures are more individualistic, while Eastern cultures are more collectivist (Bellah, 1987; Hofstede, 1983; Hong et al., 1987; Rokeach, 1973). In individualistic cultures, individual interests and goals prevail over collective interest and goals; ties between individuals are loose; and the emphasis is on the belief that individual has control of, and is responsible for, his or her own life.

The cultural value of individualism and collectivism may be manifested in the iconic image of characters in the advertisements. As indicated by Alden et al.'s 1993 study, advertising in the highly collectivist cultures of Thailand and South Korea tends to portray characters in a "group stance," compared to "individualistic stance" in advertising of highly individualistic cultures of Germany and the United States.

31

Even within different Western countries, the varying degrees of individualism may be manifested in differential iconic images of characters. Frith and Wesson's (1991) study indicated that while individualism exists in England, it is not as highly developed a national "ethos" as it is in the United States, and this is reflected in British advertising which more frequently features people in a group stance.

Cultural Differences and Indexical Feature Transfer

Cultural differences in communication style may also be reflected in indexical codification of visuals in advertising. The previous section on Linguistic Codification revealed that American direct communication style manifests itself in greater use of informational speech act and directive speech act , and lesser use of poetic speech act which utilizes indirect rhetorical devices such as verbal metaphor, simile, double meaning and the like. Indexical Feature Transfer is like a visual metaphor (Vestergaard & Schroder, 1985), but often easier to understand than verbal metaphor. Also, through the use of a visual metaphor it is possible to imply something which cannot be expressed verbally without an obvious absurdity (e.g., the previous example of the diamond ring and love). Therefore, it can be speculated that the Indexical Feature Transfer approach will be used more frequently in U.S. advertising than in advertisements of other countries where indirect rhetorical styles are more dominant. The only study examining this aspect of advertising provides support for such speculation or hypothesis. Cutler and Javalgi (1992) conducted a cross-cultural analysis of magazine advertisements in the United States, France and the United Kingdom. Their analysis of the visual content revealed that the use of association approach or indexical feature transfer was greater in U.S. advertising than in French or British advertising. Comparison between France and Britain indicated that French advertising utilized this approach more often than British advertising. On the other hand, verbal metaphorical approach was used more frequently in France and Britain than in the United States.

32

Cultural Differences and Iconic Image of Gender

Previous studies also noted that social norms about appropriate roles for women and men differ among cultures (Hawkins & Coney, 1976; Ortner, 1974). A culture's gender role norms manifest themselves in advertising (Courtney & Whipple, 1983), and advertising shapes, reinforces or perpetuates misconceptions or stereotypes about gender roles in society (Ewen & Ewen, 1982; Ferguson et al., 1990; Hawkins & Coney, 1976; Pollay, 1986; Silverstein & Silverstein, 1974).

Several studies in the United States revealed that advertising of the 1980s was still stereotypical in terms of sex role portrayals; however, the margins of difference were less than those of the 1970s (e.g., Courtney & Whipple, 1983; Gilly, 1988; Lysonski, 1983). A recent study by Klassen, Jasper and Schwartz (1993) also found that U.S. advertising still portrays women in traditional poses relative to advertisements that showed women and men together as equals, but the degree of traditional portrayals has been decreasing since the early 1980s. These studies indicated that although considerable changes have taken place within American society in terms of gender roles following the women's liberation movement, the images of the sexes in advertising are not keeping pace with the social change.

The Gilly (1988) study found that Mexican television ads were slightly more stereotypical than U.S. advertisements, and considerably more stereotypical than Australian advertisements. Some researchers noted that because the women's liberation movement was slow to develop in Mexico, women in Mexico were more traditional than American women (Navarro, 1979; Olson, 1977).

In more general terms, social scientists also noted that in most traditional cultures, the roles or behaviors of men and women are more clearly distinguished and the pressure to maintain these distinctions is quite strong (e.g., Navarro, 1979; Olson, 1977). Hofstede's (1983) typology of cultural distinctions also suggests that Eastern cultures are "high on power distance" meaning that power is more unequally distributed. The Alden et al. (1993) study examined this dimension in humorous television ads of Thailand, South Korea, the United States and Germany, and found

33

that more humorous ads portrayed unequal status between characters in Thailand and South Korea.

Combined Verbal-Visual Codification

Individualism vs. Collectivism and the Comparative Approach

In American highly individualistic culture, face-to-face competition is encouraged and "frontal attack" is an acceptable tactic (Belk & Bryce, 1986). This social value is manifested in U.S. advertising, which more frequently utilizes comparative advertising techniques (verbal and/or visual) that directly attack competitors and present its own product with that of the competitor (Cutler & Javalgi, 1992; Hong et al., 1987). In Japan, collectivism and cooperation are a socially desirable virtue, face-to-face competition is considered less desirable, and consequently, comparative advertising techniques are less utilized (e.g., Hong et al., 1987).

The foregoing literature review and conceptual analysis indicate that cultural differences are reflected in advertising strategies and expressions of different countries. Cross-cultural differences in advertising strategies and expressions were found between Western and Eastern cultures, and even between Western countries that are believed to be not very different in terms of cultural traits and level of economic development. The two cross-cultural studies which were identified involving developed and developing countries also revealed differences in advertising expressions (Gilly, 1988, Mexico & the United States; and Alden et al., 1993, Thailand, South Korea, the United States and Germany). Comparison of Rice and Lu's (1988) analysis of Chinese magazine advertising with previous studies of Western advertising also revealed significant differences. There has been no specific study of Indian advertising. However, in terms of cultural traits, India can be classified as highly collectivist, high on power distance, and a high-context culture (the researcher is from the Indian Subcontinent). This view is also well documented in the literature of sociology, cultural anthropology and international marketing (e.g., Hofstede's 1983 typology of cultural values).

34

Based on this conceptual discussion of the existing empirical evidence, the current study expected to find significant differences in advertising strategies and expressions of the United States and India in terms of (1) linguistic codification (informational, directive, poetic, expressive speech acts); (2) visual codification (iconic stance of characters, indexical value transfer, iconic image of women); and (3) combined verbal/visual codification (comparative approach).

However, the focus of this study was not whether advertising strategies and expressions differ, but how they differ, and what elements or aspects are different or similar. The answers to these questions do have important implications for international marketing and advertising practitioners because such information would be vital in formulating effective localized advertising strategies and expressions for the two countries (India & U.S.) and perhaps for other countries that are similar in terms of culture and economic/industrial development. The evidence of specific cross-cultural differences will add to the existing research findings that suggest that despite some convergence of values, norms and lifestyles in some segments of affluent consumers in many countries, diverse cultures of the world still differ on numerous points. Any evidence of similarities or differences in manifest cultural values and norms in line with or divergent from those in the West can also be used to address the question of cultural imperialism and the debates over whether and how advertising reflects, reinforces and affects cultural values of its target audience.

CHAPTER IV

METHODOLOGY

A content analysis method was utilized (with merging of some semiotic concepts) to analyze and compare the linguistic as well as visual content of a sample of U.S. and Indian national advertising campaigns for consumer products (product categories are specified and defined below) carried out in the print media.

Research Questions

This exploratory and descriptive content analysis addressed the following specific questions:

1. What are the specific linguistic and visual characteristics of magazine advertisements (as appeared in a randomly selected sample of ads) in the United States and India?

2. How do magazine advertisements in the United States and India differ in terms

3. of (a) linguistic codification (informational, directive, poetic, and expressive speech acts); (b) visual codification (iconic stance of characters, indexical value transfer, iconic image of women); and (c) combined verbal/visual codification (direct and indirect comparative approach).

Sampling and Data Collection

The population for this study was advertisements in nationally circulated news magazines and specialized business magazines of the United States and India, between January 1993 and December 1994. The national news magazines and specialized business magazines were chosen because the focus of the study was to determine similarities and differences in advertising not only between two countries but also between audiences of national news magazines and specialized business magazines within each country.

A multistage stratified sampling method was utilized for selecting a sample of advertisements. First, two comparable nationally circulated news magazines and specialized

36

business magazines were selected from each country: Time and Business Week from the United States, and India Today and Business India from India. One issue per month was selected randomly from each magazine of each country from the years 1993 and 1994.

Only ads with photographs, cartoons or true-life drawings (that portray human characters or animals) were used. Also, only full-page (single-page) advertisements were considered for this study because of their dominant use in magazines and also because this procedure controls for advertisement size. This is also a well-established standard procedure for the analysis of magazine advertising (e.g., Biswas et al., 1992; Harmon, et al., 1983).

The advertisements were stratified into three groups based on the type of product being advertised: durable goods, non-durable goods and services. In marketing, the term product refers to both goods and services and their perceived tangible and intangible attributes (Kotler, 1983; McDaniel, 1982; Schoell, 1985). Although several product classification schemes are available in marketing, the above-mentioned classification scheme is more useful in content analysis of advertising as indicated by previous studies (e.g., Boddewyn et al., 1986; Cutler & Javalgi, 1992). Non-durable goods are tangible goods that are consumed fast, normally in one or few uses, and are purchased frequently. Examples of non-durable goods include soap, deodorants, razor blades, batteries, pens, salt, sugar, beer, cigarettes, newspapers, toothpastes, napkins, over-the-counter medicines and many food products such as candy, cookies and soft drinks. Durable goods are tangible goods that normally survive long-term uses, and are not purchased as frequently. Examples include clothing, electronics and major appliances (e.g., stereo sound systems, television or radio sets, refrigerators, dishwashers, cameras), furniture and automobiles. Services are intangible activities, benefits or satisfactions that are offered for sale. Examples include insurance, banking services, repair and maintenance services, travel agencies, travel resorts, day care nurseries, health care, legal services, tax preparers, car rentals, airlines, hotels, laundries, movie theaters, beauty shops, real estate agencies and automatic car washes.

A stratified sample of advertisements was selected in the following way. First, full-page consumer product advertisements (not industrial product or business-to-business) with illustrations from each country were identified and marked in each of the selected issues of each magazine according to durable goods, non-durable goods and services. Duplication of ads was avoided by randomly marking one of the ads, when more than one ad was found for the same brand. Finally, a random sample of advertisements was selected by picking every third ad from each of the three groups of ads from each country. A total of 75 ads were randomly selected from the 24 issues (from 1993 & 1994) of each magazine (25 for durable goods, 25 for non-durable goods, 25 for services), resulting in a total of 150 ads from the two magazines of each country and a grand total of 300 ads from the two countries. Previous research indicates that for a content analysis of one or two types of magazines, such sample size is adequate (e.g., Gilly, 1988; Graham et al., 1993; Mueller, 1987). The sample is kept manageable also to get proportionate numbers of ads for consumer durables, non-durables and services. This is also a better procedure for reducing proportion oriented bias in sample, as indicated by some studies (e.g., Hong et al., 1987).

Unit of Analysis and Category System

The unit of analysis is full-page display advertisement. The variables to be analyzed are (1) linguistic codification (informational, directive, poetic, expressive speech acts); (2) visual codification (iconic stance of characters, indexical value transfer, iconic image of women); and (3) combined verbal/visual codification (direct and indirect comparative approach).

The categories for the variables to be examined were precisely defined for the coders so that different coders could apply them to the same content and reach similar conclusions. This objectivity is one of the most important criteria of a content analysis and is a significant factor in increasing the reliability of the analysis. In order to ensure that the content analysis is objective and systematic, the categories of analysis were pretested on a small sample of content for exclusivity, exhaustivity and intercoder reliability before the main content was analyzed.

38

Categories for Linguistic Codification of Advertising

Informational Speech Act or Informational Cues

In advertising, informativeness refers to the extent to which an ad focuses on consumers' practical, functional or utilitarian need for the product so that customers are able to make a sound choice between products or brands (Belch & Belch, 1990; Resnick & Stern, 1977).

Informational cues in advertisements were measured using the well-established Resnik and Stern information classification system (Resnik & Stern, 1977), with some modifications: in the price-value definition, information about saving money is included; availability included information on the varieties available; quality and performance were combined into one category because of overlap; the definition of performance included convenience in use and results of using; the definition of new ideas included new uses, improvements and new features. In addition to these modifications, examples were included to facilitate clear understanding by the coders. These categories are operationally defined as follows:

Price-Value. Does the ad provide information about the price or value of the product or service? Does it refer to the amount the consumer must pay for the product or service (this may be in absolute terms, such as a suggested retail price, or in relative terms, such as a "30% off sale," "better quality at a low price" or "best value for the dollar")?

Quality/Performance. Does the ad provide information about the attributes and characteristics of the product or service? Does it refer to how good the product or service is (may refer to craftsmanship, engineering, workmanship, durability, excellence of materials, structural superiority, superiority of personnel, special services, attention to detail, etc.)? Does the ad provide any information about how well the product or service perform, convenience in use, or about results of using it (for example, "gives hair bounce," "will not yellow floors," "user friendly," "whiter teeth," "leaves you feeling fresh all day")?

Components. Does the ad provide information about the components or ingredients of the products or any ancillary items included with the product (for example, "contains baking soda," or "the only toothpaste with stannous fluoride")?
Availability. When, where and how many varieties of the product is available for purchase (for example, "now available in supermarkets," or "not available in all areas," or "available in six different colors")?

<u>Taste.</u> Is any testimony by a sample of potential customers presented to substantiate the claim of superior taste?

<u>Nutrition.</u> Are there any data presented regarding the nutritional characteristics of the product (for example, "fortified with vitamin D")?

<u>Special Offers.</u> Does the ad provide information about limited-time non-price deals such as two-for-one deals, rebates, premiums?

<u>Packaging or Shape.</u> Does the ad provide information about special packaging or shape of the product that makes it superior than alternative products (for example, "package is reusable," "special two in one package")?

<u>Safety.</u> Does the ad provide information about safety features of the product (for example, "built-in cut-off switch," or "will not harm delicate hair")?

<u>Warranties and Guarantees.</u> Does the ad provide information about post-purchase assurances (for example, "All-service five-year warranty," or "money-back guarantee")?

<u>Independent Research.</u> Does the ad provide information concerning research/tests about the product conducted by an independent research organization?

<u>Company Sponsored Research.</u> Does the ad provide information concerning company's own research data about the product?

<u>New ideas/New uses/Improvements or New Features.</u> Is a new concept or new way to use the existing product introduced in the commercial? Are its advantages presented? Is there any improved feature of the existing product? For example, "use Acme baking soda to deodorize refrigerator," "new, milder...," "now with 50% less sugar."

Mandatory information, such as warning labels required by the government, were not counted as information cues. The informativeness of an advertisement was viewed as a continuum--from low to high--zero to seven or more information cues. An advertisement low in informational content is operationally defined as one with zero to one information cues. An advertisement high in informational content is operationally defined as one that contains four or more information cues, and an advertisement moderate in informational content is operationally defined as one containing two to three information cues.

<u>Expressive Speech Act, Directive Speech Act, Poetic Speech Act</u>

Based on Vestergaard and Schroder's (1985) linguistic classification of speech acts in advertising, these categories are operationally defined as follows:

<u>Expressive Speech Act.</u> Does the advertisement talk about the company? For example, does the ad identify and praise the company and recommend its product (e.g. "another fine product from Proctor & Gamble")? Does the ad condemn or criticize its competitors? Does it apologize for inconvenience caused by a faulty part or other problems?

<u>Directive Speech Act.</u> Are the potential consumers directly asked to do something or think about something (for example, "try X"; "get X"; "use X"; "ask/call for details"; " give her an X"; "introduce your family to X"; "look for X at your department store"; "contact your dealer"; "come to our showroom")?

<u>Poetic Speech Act.</u> Does the advertisement utilize poetic devices or indirect rhetorical devices such as rhyme, metaphor, simile, double meaning, philosophic or euphemistic expressions, etc.?

Categories for Visual Codification of Advertising

<u>Iconic Stance of Characters</u>

Based on Frith and Wesson's (1991) category scheme and Alden et al.'s (1993) scheme, two categories were used to measure this variable.

Individualistic Stance. Does the advertisement feature just one or two individuals?

Collective Stance. Does the advertisement feature three or more people in a group context?

<u>Indexical Feature Transfer</u>

Vestergaard and Schoder's (1985) original semiotic definition of indexical feature transfer was applied to measure three categories. According to the original definition, indexical feature transfer occurs in advertising when the product is associated with persons or situations whose desirable attributes are well known. The three categories are operationally defined as follows:

41

Physical Attractiveness Attribute. Does the advertisement try to establish an indexical relation between the product and physical attractiveness attribute of a person (whether a model or a real-life celebrity)? In other words, is the product associated with the physical attractiveness of a person (for example, the product is shown with physically attractive models or real-life celebrities)?

Sophistication/Status Attribute. Does the advertisement try to establish an indexical relation between the product and sophistication/high status by associating the product with wealthy and powerful people (for example, the ad shows the product being used by wealthy and powerful people)?

Loving/Caring Attribute. Does the advertisement try to establish an indexical relation between the product and love/care by associating the product with people in a loving/caring situation (for example, a diamond ring is shown with a couple in a romantic situation; individuals are shown in a loving/caring situation with parents, children or friends, and the product is shown as a gift or as a token of love/care)?

Iconic Image of Women

This variable was measured by the following categories based on the classification

schemes developed by Cutler and Javalgi (1992); Stewart and Furse (1986); Courtney &

Lockerretz (1971); Schneider and Schneider (1979); Poe (1976); and Alden et al. (1993).

Traditional, Stereotypical, Unequal Portrayal. To what extent does the ad portray a stereotypical image of women (on a 5-point scale ranging from entirely non-stereotypical to highly stereotypical)?

A highly stereotypical portrayal is where women are shown in (a) traditional, stereotypical roles and (b) unequal status. For example, (a) women are shown as housewife, mother, girlfriend, date or in traditional female occupation such as secretary, nurse, hairdresser; or (b) women are shown as passive, submissive, recipients of help, advice or order, not powerful, not wealthy. If only one condition (a or b) is met then circle 4 on the 5-point scale.

An entirely non-stereotypical portrayal is where women are shown in (a) non-traditional roles and (b) equal status. For example, (a) women are shown as professionals, high level executives, authority figures; or (b) women are shown as active, aggressive, assertive, givers of help, advice or order, wealthy, powerful. If only one condition (a or b) is met then circle 2 on the 5-point scale.

A neutral portrayal is where the role is not clearly identifiable.

Physical Exploitation/Portrayal as Sex Object. To what extent does the exploit women's bodies and portray women as sex objects (on a 5-point scale ranging from no exploitation to high exploitation)?

A very high exploitation ad (a) focuses on the physical attributes of women's bodies. Camera focuses and exhibits specific attributes of the body; (b) women are scantily clad/wearing skimpy sexy clothing while men are fully clothed; and (c) women are portrayed as the object of explicit male gaze. If all three conditions are met then circle 5. If two conditions are met then circle 4. If only one condition is met then circle 3 or 2 depending on how negative the portrayal is.

Categories for Combined Verbal-Visual Codification

Comparative Approach

Based on Stewart and Furse's (1986) category scheme, this variable was measured by three categories which are operationally defined as follows:

Explicit or Direct Comparison. Is the product compared (visually and/or verbally) with competitor's product and is the competitor and/or its brand identified by name?

Implicit or Indirect Comparison. Is a comparison made between the advertised product and a competitor without identifying the competitor by name (for example, "compared to the leading brand")?

Puffery or Unsubstantiated Claim. Is the product declared best, better, finest without substantiation or identification of attribute?

Coding Procedures and Reliability Tests

A content analysis is considered reliable when repeated measurement of the same material leads to similar conclusions or results (Wimmer & Dominick, 1991). Reliability is the ability of a measurement system to generate consistent results each time it is used (Monette et al., 1986). In order to determine if the categorization and quantification system and coding instruments are reliable, intercoder reliability tests were performed. Intercoder reliability refers to levels of agreement among independent coders who conduct the coding of the same content using the same coding instruments.

Two coders were employed to evaluate the sample of ads. The two coders were trained and familiarized with the precise definitions of categories and coding instruments. Detailed instruction sheets were made available that clearly explained categorization and quantification systems and provided examples for coding. Trial runs were conducted so that a common frame of reference could develop between coders. During these trial runs, any causes of disagreements were identified and resolved.

The intercoder reliability was measured by two tests. First, a small sample (24%) of the U.S. and Indian advertisements were randomly selected for a pretest. Then the two coders were asked to code the same pretest sample of advertisements using the same coding instruments. Responses of the coders were compared item by item and the numbers of agreement were determined. Intercoder reliability was then tested using the Holsti's reliability formula (Holsti, 1969). The reliability test results were within the acceptable levels (.94 for information cues, .90 for speech acts, .92 for comparative approach, .96 for iconic stance, .90 for indexical feature transfer, .90 for image of women). The main sample of ads was then randomly assigned to the two coders. When the coding was complete, a subsample (24%) of the data was reanalyzed by independent coders. Intercoder reliability was then tested using the Holsti's reliability formula (Holsti, 1969). The reliability test results were again within the acceptable levels (ranging from reliability coefficients of .90 to .96). To account for the element of chance in coder agreement, all tests were recalculated using Scott's pi formula (Scott, 1969). The reliability test results for all items were again within acceptable levels (above .75).

Data Analysis and Statistical Test

The data were analyzed by SPSSx. Nominal level data measurements such as frequency counts and valid percentages were used for all but two variables. Interval level data measurements such as calculations of means were used for (a) total number of information cues used, and (b) images of women. To test if the variables (generating nominal level data) are significantly different between U.S. and Indian advertising campaigns, chi-square tests and

44

Spearman's rho tests were performed. To test if the variables (generating interval level data) were significantly different, t tests and ANOVA tests were performed. Each variable was tested independently for country differences. In addition, each variable was also tested for country differences within the durable goods, non-durable goods and service categories. This procedure was necessary because advertising often differs according to product categories and it is wise to control for product category in cross-cultural studies (e.g., Boddewyn et al., 1986; Cutler & Javalgi, 1992). Although no differences were expected in the variables in terms of two different magazines in each country, tests were performed nevertheless to ensure that it was not necessary to test each variable independently between similar magazines of the two countries.

CHAPTER V

RESULTS

The data analysis revealed that there are significant differences in many aspects of advertising strategies and expressions in India and the United States.

The results will be presented, first, in terms of each variable by country (comparison between countries regardless of type of magazine or type of product). This will be followed by an analysis of each variable by country across product category. Finally, an analysis of each variable by type of product and type of magazine within each country will be presented. An analysis of each variable by type of magazine within each individual country did not show significant difference for any variable, and therefore, no comparisons were made between countries by type of magazine.

Information Content in Advertising

Information Content (by Country)

Table 1 presents a comparison of various information cues between the two countries. The analysis revealed that there was significant difference in the use of only two types of information cues. The results showed that "availability information" cue was more utilized by Indian advertisements than by their U.S. counterparts. About 53% of the Indian ads used availability information cue, whereas only 10% of the U.S. ads contained availability information cue. A chi-square test showed that the difference was statistically significant (X^2=65.08, df=1, p<.001). The results also revealed that "company-sponsored research" information was more utilized by U.S. ads than their Indian counterparts. About 10% of the U.S. ads used this information cue, whereas only .7% of the Indian ads contained this information cue. A Chi Square analysis showed that the difference was statistically significant (X^2=12.94, df=1, p<.001).

Although some differences were found in the use of other information cues, chi-square analysis indicated that these differences were not statistically significant.

Table 1   Use of Information Cues (by Country)

Type of Information	U.S. Ads	Indian Ads	
Availability Info Cue	15 (10%)	80 (53%)	X^2=65.08; df=1; p<.001
Quality/Performance	128 (85%)	129 (86%)	X^2=.02, df=1, p=.86
Components	44(29%)	33 (22%)	X^2=2.11, df=1, p=.14
Price/Value	· 22 (15%)	18 (12%)	X^2=.46, df=1, p=.49
Safety	17 (11%)	17 (11%)	X^2=.00, df=1, p=1.00
New Ideas/Features	8 (5%)	10 (7%)	X^2=.23, df=1, p=.62
Nutrition	7 (5%)	2 (1%)	X^2=2.86, df=1, p=.09
Special Offers	6 (4%)	3 (2%)	X^2=1.03, df=1, p=.30
Warranties/Guaranties	7(5%)	2 (1%)	X^2=2.86, df=1, p=.09
Company Research	15 (10%)	1(.7%)	X^2=12.94, df=1, p<.001

Chi-square tests were not performed on the following information cues because 75% of the cells did not have 5 or more observations and each cell did not have at least one observation. (current statistical rule of thumb, Schulman, 1992; Spatz & Johnston, 1984).

Packaging	1 (.7%)	1 (.7)
Taste	2 (1%) 0	
Ind. Research	8 (5%) 0	

In both Indian and U.S. ads, quality/performance information was the most commonly used cue. In U.S. ads, the second most frequently used information cue was components/ingredients, while in Indian ads, the second most common information cue was availability information. A Spearman's rho test for the ranking of all 13 information cues, however, indicated no significant difference in the importance of various information cues between the two countries (r_s=.75; p<.05).

Table 2 presents the mean number of information cues by country. The results indicated that U.S. ads had a mean information score of 1.87 and the Indian ads had a mean score of 1.98. A t test indicated that the difference was not statistically significant (t=-.84; df=298; p=.40). It is therefore concluded that on average Indian and U.S. ads contain similar number of information cues.

Table 2   Mean Information Cues (by Country)

Country	Mean	
U.S.	1.87	(n=150)
Indian	1.98	(n=150)

t=-.84; df=298; p=.40

The analysis was also broken down into low level of information (0-1 information cues), medium level of information (2-3 information cues) and high levels of information (4-7 information cues). Table 3 presents the number and percentages of advertisements containing varying levels of information cues. The results revealed that a larger percentage of U.S. ads (45%) had a low level of information cues compared to 30% for Indian advertisements. Also, a slightly larger percentage of U.S. ads (9%) contained a high level of information cues compared to 8% for Indian advertisements. On the other hand, a larger percentage of Indian ads (62%) had a medium level of information cues compared to 46% for U.S. advertisements. A chi- square analysis, however, did not find any statistical significance.

48

Table 3   Level of Information (by Country)

Level of Information	U.S. Ads	Indian Ads
Low Level	67 (45%, n=150)	45 (30%, n=150)
Medium Level	69 (46%, n=150)	93 (62%, n=150)
High Level	14 (9%, n=150)	12 (8%, n=150)

$X^2=8.03$; df=2; p=.01

Information Content (by Type of Product, Between Countries)

When the variable "information cue" was analyzed by type of product, the results found significant differences for several information cues.

Table 4 presents a comparison of various information cues in durable product ads of the two countries. The analysis revealed that availability information cue was more utilized by Indian ads than by their U.S. counterparts. The results indicated that only 12% of the U.S. ads used the "availability" information cue, whereas 60% of the Indian ads contained this information cue. A chi-square analysis showed that the difference was statistically significant ($X^2=25.00$, df=1, p<.001). The analysis also revealed that the "price/value" information cue was more utilized by the U.S. durable ads than the Indian durable ads. The results indicated that 32% of the U.S. durable ads used the "price/value" information cue whereas only 10% of the Indian durable ads contained this information cue. A Chi Square analysis showed that the difference was statistically significant ($X^2=7.29$, df=1, p<.01).

For durable product ads, the use of other information cues was not found to be significantly different between the two countries.

Table 4   Use of Information Cues (Durable Product Ads)

Type of Information	U.S. Ads	Indian Ads	
Availability Info Cue	6 (12%)	30 (60%)	X^2=25.00; d.f.=1; p<.001
Price/Value	16 (32%)	5 (10%)	X^2=65.08; d.f.=1; p<.001
Quality/Performance	48 (96%)	45 (90%)	X^2=1.38, df=1, p=.23
Components	20 (40%)	11 (22%)	X^2=3.78, df=1, p=.05
Warranties/Guaranties	5(10%)	1 (2%)	X^2=2.83, df=1, p=.09
Safety	4 (8%)	7 (14%)	X^2=.91, df=1, p=.33
New Ideas/Features	2 (4%)	5 (10%)	X^2=1.38, df=1, p=.23

Chi square tests were not performed on the following information cues because 75% of the cells did not have 5 or more observations and each cell did not have at least one observation. (current statistical rule of thumb, Schulman, 1992; Spatz & Johnston 1984).

Independent Research	2 (4%)	0
Company Research	1 (2%)	0
Special Offers	1 (2%)	0
Nutrition	0	0
Packaging	0	0
Taste	0	0

Table 5 presents the mean number of information cues by durable product. The results indicate that the U.S. ads had a mean information score of 1.70 and the Indian ads had a mean score of 1.82. A t test indicated that the difference was not statistically significant (t=-.99, df=98, p=.32). It is therefore concluded that Indian and U.S. ads for durable products contain a similar number of information cues on the average.

Table 5   Mean Information Cues (Durable Product Ads)

Country	Mean	
U.S.	1.70	(n=50)
Indian	1.82	(n=50)

t=-.99, df=98, p=.32

Table 6 presents a comparison of various information cues in non-durable product ads of the two countries. The analysis revealed that the availability information cue was utilized more by Indian non-durable ads than by their U.S. counterparts. The results indicate that only 10% of the U.S. non-durable ads used the "availability" information cue whereas 38% of the Indian non-durable ads contained this information cue. A chi-square analysis showed that the difference was statistically significant (X^2=10.74, df=1, p=.001).

The analysis also revealed that "company research" information cue was more utilized by the U.S. non-durable ads than the Indian non-durable ads. The results indicated that 26% of the U.S. non-durable ads used "company research" information cue whereas only 2% of Indian non-durable ads contained this information cue. A chi-square analysis showed that the difference was statistically significant (X^2=11.96, df=1, p<.001).

For non-durable product ads, the use of other information cues was not found to be significantly different.

Table 6   Use of Information Cues (Non-Durable Product Ads)

Type of Information	U.S. Ads	Indian Ads	
Availability Info	5 (10%)	19 (38%)	X^2=10.74, df=1, p=.001
Quality/Performance	38 (76%)	37 (74%)	X^2=.05, df=1, p=.81
Components	19 (38%)	11 (22%)	X^2=3.04, df=1, p=.08
Safety	9 (18%)	7 (14%)	X^2=.29, df=1, p=.58
Company Research	13 (26%)	1 (2%)	X^2=11.96, df=1, p<.001
Nutrition	7 (14%)	2 (4%)	X^2=3.05, df=1, p=.08

Chi-square tests were not performed on the following information cues because 75% of the cells did not have 5 or more observations and each cell did not have at least one observation. (current statistical rule of thumb, Schulman, 1992; Spatz & Johnston, 1984).

New Ideas/Features	2 (4%)	4 (8%)
Special Offers	2 (4%)	2 (4%)
Taste	2 (4%)	0
Independent Research	1(2%)	0
Packaging	0	1 (2%)
Price	0	0
Warranties/Guaranties	0	0

Table 7 presents the mean number of information cues by non-durable product. The results indicate that the U.S. ads had a mean information score of 1.74 and the Indian ads had a mean score of 1.66. A t test indicated that the difference was not statistically significant (t=.59; df=98; p=.55). It is therefore concluded that Indian and U.S. non-durable ads contain a similar number of information cues.

Table 7   Mean Information Cues (Non-Durable Product Ads)

Country	Mean	
U.S.	1.74	(n=50)
Indian	1.66	(n=50)

t=.59; df=98; p=.55

Table 8 presents a comparison of various information cues in service ads of the two countries. The analysis revealed that, as in durable and non-durable product ads, the availability information cue was utilized more by the Indian service ads than their U.S. counterparts. The results indicated that only 8% of the U.S. service ads used the "availability" information cue whereas 62% of the Indian service ads contained this information cue. A chi-square analysis showed that the difference was statistically significant (X^2=32.04; df=1; p<.001). For service ads, the use of other information cues was not found to be significantly different.

Table 8   Use of Information Cues (Service Ads)

Type of Information	U.S. Ads	Indian Ads	
Availability Info	5 (10%)	31 (62%)	X^2=32.04; df=1; p<.001
Quality/Performance	42 (84%)	47 (94%)	X^2=2.55; df=1; p=.11
Price/value	6 (12%)	13 (26%)	X^2=3.18; df=1; p=.07
Components	5 (10%)	11 (22%)	X^2=2.67; df=1; p=.10

Chi-square tests were not performed on the following information cues because 75% of the cells did not have 5 or more observations and each cell did not have at least one observation. (current statistical rule of thumb, Schulman, 1992; Spatz & Johnston, 1984).

Independent Research	5 (10%)	0 (n=50)
Safety	4 (8%)	3 (6%)
New Ideas/Features	4 (8%)	1 (2%)
Special Offers	3 (6%)	1 (2%
Warranties/Guaranties	2 (4%)	1 (2%)

Table 9 presents the mean number of information cues for service ads. The results indicate that the Indian service ads had comparatively more information cues per ad. The U.S. ads had a mean information score of 1.50 and the Indian ads had a mean score of 1.86. A t test indicated that the difference was statistically significant (t=-3.34; df= 98; p=.001).

Table 9   Mean Information Cues (Service Ads)

Country	Mean	
U.S.	1.50	(n=50)
Indian	1.86	(n=50)

t=-3.34; df= 98; p=.001

Information Content (by Type of Product, Within Country)

When the information content of advertising within each country was analyzed by type of product, the results showed statistically significant differences for only a few types of information cues. The use of most information cues did not vary within each individual country across product categories.

Table 10 presents the number and percentages of U.S. durable, non-durable and service advertisements using various types of information cues.

Table 10   Information Cues (U.S. Ads by Type of Product)

Info Cue	Durable	Non-Durable	Service	
Quality	48 (96%, n=50)	38 (76%, n=50)	42 (84%, n=50)	X^2=8.09; df=2; p=.01
Component	20 (40%, n=50)	19 (38%, n=50)	5 (10%, n=50)	X^2=13.57; df=2; p<.001
Availability	6 (12%, n=50)	5 (10%, n=50)	5 (10%, n=50)	X^2=.44; df=2; p=.80

Chi square tests were not performed on the following information cues because 75% of the cells did not have 5 or more observations and each cell did not have at least one observation. (current statistical rule of thumb, Schulman, 1992; Spatz & Johnston, 1984).

(table continues)

55

Price/value	16 (32%, n=50)	0 (n=50)	6 (12%, n=50)
Taste	0 (n=50)	2 (4%, n=50)	0 (n=50)
Safety	4 (8%, n=50)	9 (18%, n=50)	4 (8%, n=50)
New Ideas	2 (4%, n=50)	2 (4%, n=50)	4 (8%, n=50)
Special Offer	1 (2%, n=50)	2 (4%, n=50)	3 (6%, n=50)
Warranties	5 (10%, n=50)	0 (n=50)	2 (4%, n=50)
Ind Research	2 (4%, n=50)	1 (2%, n=50)	5 (10%, n=50)
Company Res	1 (2%, n=50)	13 (26%, n=50)	1 (2%, n=50)
Packaging	0 (n=50)	0 (n=50)	1 (2%, n=50)
Nutrition	0 (n=50)	7 (14%, n=50)	0 (n=50)

The results showed statistical significance for only one type of information cue (components). The use of this information cue varies according to durable product, non-durable product and service advertisements within the U.S. ads. Durable product advertisements were likely to place more emphasis on the component information cue than non-durable product and service advertisements.

Table 11 compares the mean number of information cues for durable product, non-durable product and service advertisements in the United States. An ANOVA test indicated that the difference was statistically nonsignificant ($F=.82$; $df=2$, 149; $p=.43$). It is therefore concluded that U.S. durable product, non-durable product and service advertisements were similar in terms of mean number of information cues.

Table 11   Mean Information Cues (U.S. Ads by Type of Product)

Type of Product	Mean	
Durable Product Ads	1.60	(n=50)
Non-Durable Product Ads	1.58	(n=50)
Service Ads	1.48	(n=50)

F=.82; df=2, 149; p=.43

Table 12 presents the number and percentages of Indian durable, non-durable and service advertisements using various types of information cues.

Table 12   Information Cues (Indian Ads by Type of Product)

Info Cue	Durable	Non-Durable	Service	
Quality	45 (90%, n=50)	37 (74%, n=50)	47 (94%, n=50)	X^2=9.30; df=2; p<.01
Component	11 (22%, n=50)	11 (22%, n=50)	11 (22%, n=50)	X^2=.00; df=2; p=1.00
Availability	30 (60%, n=50)	19 (38%, n=50)	31 (62%, n=50)	X^2=7.12; df=2; p=.02
Safety	7 (14%, n=50)	7 (14%, n=50)	3 (6%, n=50)	X^2=2.12; df=2; p=.34

Chi-square tests were not performed on the following information cues because 75% of the cells did not have 5 or more observations and each cell did not have at least one observation. (current statistical rule of thumb, Schulman, 1992; Spatz & Johnston, 1984).

Price/value	5 (10%, n=50)	0 (n=50)	13 (26%, n=50)
New Ideas	5 (10%, n=50)	4 (8%, n=50)	1 (2%, n=50)

(table continues)

Special Offer	0 (n=50)	2 (4%, n=50)	1 (2%, n=50)
Warranties	1 (2%, n=50)	0 (n=50)	1 (2%, n=50)
Company Res	0 (n=50)	1 (2%, n=50)	0 (n=50)
Ind Research	0 (n=50)	0 (n=50)	0 (n=50)
Taste	0 (n=50)	0 (n=50)	0 (n=50)
Packaging	0 (n=50)	1 (2%, n=50)	0 (n=50)
Nutrition	0 (n=50)	2 (4%, n=50)	0 (n=50)

The results showed statistical significance for only one information cue (quality). The use of this information cue varies according to durable product, non-durable product and service advertisements within the Indian ads. Durable and Service advertisements were likely to emphasize the quality information cue than non-durable product advertisements.

Table 13 compares the mean number of information cues for durable product, non-durable product and service advertisements in India. An ANOVA test indicated that the difference was statistically nonsignificant ($F=2.71$; $df=2$, 149; $p=.07$).

Table 13   Mean Information Cues (Indian Ads by Type of Product)

Type of Product	Mean	
Durable Product Ads	1.74	(n=50)
Non-Durable Product Ads	1.58	(n=50)
Service Ads	1.78	(n=50)

$F=2.71$; $df=2$, 149; $p=.07$

58

Information Content (by Type of Magazine, Within Country)

When the information content of advertising within each country was analyzed by type of magazine, the results showed that the use of information cues did not differ significantly within each individual country across two magazine categories (news magazine and business magazine).

Table 14 presents the number and percentages of advertisements in two U.S. magazines using various types of information cues. The results indicated that there was no statistically significant difference in the use of information cues in advertising of the two U.S. magazines.

Table 14   Information Cues (U.S. Ads by Type of Magazine)

Info Cue	Time	Business Week	
Price/value	9 (12%, n=75)	13 (17%, n=75)	$X^2=.85$; df=1; p=.35
Component	27 (36%, n=75)	17 (23%, n=75)	$X^2=3.21$; df=1; p=.07
Availability	10 (13%, n=75)	5 (7%, n=75)	$X^2=1.85$; df=1; p=.17
Quality	58 (77%, n=75)	70 (93%, n=75)	$X^2=7.67$; df=1; p=.06
Safety	6 (8%, n=75)	11 (15%, n=75)	$X^2=1.65$; df=1; p=.19
Company Res	7 (9%, n=75)	8 (11%, n=75)	$X^2=.07$; df=1; p=.78
Ind Research	6 (8%, n=75)	2 (3%, n=75)	$X^2=2.11$; df=1; p=.14

Chi-square tests were not performed on the following information cues because 75% of the cells did not have 5 or more observations and each cell did not have at least one observation. (current statistical rule of thumb, Schulman, 1992; Spatz & Johnston, 1984).

(table continues)

Taste	2 (3%, n=75)	0 (n=75)
New Ideas	4 (5%, n=75)	4 (5%, n=75)
Special Offer	6 (8%, n=75)	0 (n=75)
Warranties	3 (4%, n=75)	4 (5%, n=75)
Packaging	1 (1%, n=75)	0 (n=75)
Nutrition	0 (n=75)	7 (9%, n=75)

Table 15 presents the mean number of information cues in the two U.S. magazines. A t test indicated that the difference was statistically non-significant (t=.02; df=148; p=.87). It is therefore concluded that advertisements in the two U.S. magazines were similar in terms of mean number of information cues.

Table 15   Mean Information Cues (U.S. Ads by Type of Magazine)

Type of Magazine	Mean	
Time	1.56	(n=75)
Business Week	1.55	(n=75)

t=.16; df=148; p=.87

Table 16 presents the number and percentages of advertisements in two Indian magazines using various types of information cues. The results indicated that there was no statistically significant difference in the use of information cues in advertising of the two Indian magazines.

60

Table 16   Information Cues (Indian Ads by Type of Magazine)

Info Cue	India Today	Business India	
Price/value	10 (13%, n=75)	8 (11%, n=75)	$X^2=.25$; df=1; p=.61
Component	21 (28%, n=75)	12 (16%, n=75)	$X^2=3.14$; df=1; p=.07
Availability	39 (52%, n=75)	41 (55%, n=75)	$X^2=.10$; df=1; p=.74
Quality	61 (81%, n=75)	68 (91%, n=75)	$X^2=2.71$; df=1; p=.09
Safety	11 (15%, n=75)	6 (8%, n=75)	$X^2=1.65$; df=1; p=.19
New Ideas	3 (4%, n=75)	7 (9%, n=75)	$X^2=1.71$; df=1; p=.19

Chi-square tests were not performed on the following information cues because 75% of the cells did not have 5 or more observations and each cell did not have at least one observation. (current statistical rule of thumb, Schulman, 1992; Spatz & Johnston, 1984).

Special Offer	2 (3%, n=75)	1 (1%, n=75)
Warranties	2 (3%, n=75)	0 (n=75)
Company Res	1 (1%, n=75)	0 (n=75)
Packaging	1 (1%, n=75)	0 (n=75)
Nutrition	1 (1%, n=75)	1 (1%, n=75)
Taste	0 (n=75)	0 (n=75)
Ind Research	0 (n=75)	0 (n=75)

Table 17 presents the mean number of information cues in the two Indian magazines. A t test indicated that the difference was statistically nonsignificant (t=1.55; df=148; p=.21). It is concluded that ads in the two Indian magazines were similar in terms of mean information cues.

Table 17   Mean Information Cues (Indian Ads by Type of Magazine)

Type of Magazine	Mean	
India Today	1.65	(n=75)
Business India	1.75	(n=75)

t=-1.25; df=148; p=.21

Speech Acts in Advertising

Speech Acts in Advertising (by Country)

The analysis of the three variables of "Speech Acts" revealed that there was significant difference in the use of different types of speech acts in advertisements of the two countries.

Table 18 presents the number and percentages of advertisements using different types of "speech acts." The analysis revealed that the U.S. ads used the expressive speech acts more often than did the Indian ads. The results indicate that 65% of the U.S. ads used the expressive speech acts while 45% of the Indian ads contained the expressive speech acts. A chi-square analysis showed that the difference was statistically significant (X^2=12.13, df=1, p<.001).

Table 18   Use of Different Speech Acts (by Country)

Speech Acts	U.S. Ads	Indian Ads	
Expressive	98 (65%, n=150)	68 (45%, n=150)	X^2=12.13; d.f.=1; p<.001
Directive	91 (61%, n=150)	71 (47%, n=150)	X^2=5.36; d.f.=1; p<.05
Poetic	14 (9%, n=150)	49 (33%, n=150)	X^2=24.61; d.f.=1; p<.001

The analysis revealed that the U.S. ads also used the directive speech acts more often than did the Indian ads. The results indicate that 61% of the U.S. ads used the directive speech acts while 47% of the Indian ads contained the directive speech acts. A chi-square analysis showed that the difference was significant ($X^2=5.36$, df=1, p<.05).

The analysis also revealed that Indian ads used the poetic speech acts more often than did the U.S. ads. The results indicated that only 9% of the U.S. ads used the poetic speech acts while 33% of the Indian ads contained this type of speech acts. A chi-square analysis showed that the difference was statistically significant ($X^2=24.61$, df=1, p<.001).

Speech Acts in Advertising (by Type of Product, Between Countries)

The two countries also differed in the use of speech acts across different product categories. When the variable "speech acts" in advertising between the two countries was analyzed by type of product, the results showed statistically significant differences for several categories.

Table 19 presents the number and percentages of durable product advertisements using different types of "speech acts" in the two countries. The analysis revealed that the tendency that was found for the use of speech acts between the two countries (regardless of type of product) also held across durable product category. That is, the U.S. durable product ads used the expressive speech acts and the directive speech acts more often than did the Indian durable product ads. On the other hand, Indian durable product ads used the poetic speech acts more often than those in the U.S. ads. A chi- square analysis showed that the differences were statistically significant.

Table 19   Use of Different Speech Acts (Durable Product Ads)

Speech Acts	U.S. Ads	Indian Ads	
Expressive	40 (80%, n=50)	23 (46%, n=50)	X^2=12.39; d.f.=1; p<.001
Directive	34 (68%, n=50)	21 (42%, n=50)	X^2=6.82; d.f.=1; p<.05
Poetic	4 (8%, n=50)	25 (50%, n=50)	X^2=21.41; d.f.=1; p<.001

The results indicate that 80% of the U.S. durable product ads used expressive speech acts while 46% of the Indian durable product ads contained expressive speech acts. Also, 68% of the U.S. durable product ads used directive speech acts while only 42% of Indian durable product ads did use this. On the other hand, only 8% of the U.S. durable product ads used poetic speech acts while 50% of the Indian ads contained these types of speech acts. A chi-square analysis showed that the differences were statistically significant at .001, .05 and .001 level respectively.

Table 20 presents the number and percentages of non-durable product advertisements using different types of "speech acts" in the two countries. The analysis revealed that the two countries also differed in the use of one type of speech acts (poetic speech acts) in non-durable product ads. Indian non-durable product ads used poetic speech acts more often than did the U.S. ads in this category. No statistically significant difference was found for the use of expressive and directive speech acts.

Table 20   Use of Different Speech Acts (Non-Durable Product Ads)

Speech Acts	U.S. Ads	Indian Ads	
Expressive	16 (32%, n=50)	15 (30%, n=50)	X^2=.04; d.f.=1; p=.82
Directive	23 (46%, n=50)	19 (38%, n=50)	X^2=.65; d.f.=1; p=.41
Poetic	2 (4%, n=50)	13 (26%, n=50)	X^2=9.49; d.f.=1; p<.01

The results indicate that only 4% of the U.S. non-durable product ads used poetic speech acts while 26% of the Indian ads contained these acts. A chi-square analysis showed that the difference was statistically significant at .01 level. On the other hand, 32% of the U.S. non-durable product ads used expressive speech acts while 30% of the Indian non-durable product ads contained these acts, and 46% of the U.S. non-durable product ads used directive speech acts while 38% of the Indian ads contained these acts in the non-durable category. A chi-square analysis showed that these differences were not statistically significant.

Table 21 presents the number and percentages of service advertisements using different types of "speech acts" in the two countries. The data analysis revealed that the U.S. service ads used expressive speech acts more often than did the Indian ads.

Table 21   Use of Different Speech Acts (Service Ads)

Speech Acts	U.S. Ads	Indian Ads	
Expressive	42 (84%, n=50)	30 (60%, n=50)	X^2=7.14; d.f.=1; p<.01
Directive	34 (68%, n=50)	31 (62%, n=50)	X^2=.39; d.f.=1; p=.52
Poetic	8 (16%, n=50)	11 (22%, n=50)	X^2=.58; d.f.=1; p=.44

The results indicate that only 84% of the U.S. service ads used expressive speech acts while 60% of the Indian ads utilized these acts. A chi-square analysis showed that the difference was statistically significant at .01 level. On the other hand, 68% of the U.S. service ads used directive speech acts while 62% of the Indian ads contained these, and 16% of the U.S. service ads used poetic speech acts while 22% of the Indian service ads contained these. A Chi square analysis showed that these differences were not statistically significant.

Speech Acts in Advertising (by Type of Product, Within Country)

When the variable "speech acts" in advertising within each country was analyzed by type of product, the results did not show statistically significant differences for most of the categories.

65

Table 22 presents the number and percentages of U.S. durable, non-durable and service ads using various types of speech acts.

Table 22   Speech Acts in Advertising (U.S. Ads by Type of Product)

Speech Act	Durable	Non-Durable	Service	
Expressive	40 (80%, n=50)	16 (32%, n=50)	42 (84%, n=50)	$X^2=36.97$; df=2; p<.001
Directive	34 (68%, n=50)	23 (46%, n=50)	34 (68%, n=50)	$X^2=6.76$; df=2; p=.03
Poetic	4 (8%, n=50)	2 (4%, n=50)	8 (16%, n=50)	$X^2=4.41$; df=2; p=.11

The results showed statistical significance for only one category (expressive speech acts). The use of directive and poetic speech acts did not seem to vary according to durable product, non-durable product and service advertisements within the United States. The use of only "expressive speech acts" was found to vary. This type of speech acts was used more often by durable and service ads than non-durable product ads.

Table 23 presents the number and percentages of Indian durable, non-durable and service advertisements using various types of speech acts.

Table 23   Speech Acts in Advertising (Indian Ads by Type of Product)

Speech Act	Durable	Non-Durable	Service	
Expressive	23 (46%, n=50)	15 (30%, n=50)	30 (60%, n=50)	$X^2=9.09$; df=2; p<.05
Directive	21 (42%, n=50)	19 (38%, n=50)	31 (62%, n=50)	$X^2=6.63$; df=2; p<.05
Poetic	25 (50%, n=50)	13 (26%, n=50)	11 (22%, n=50)	$X^2=10.42$; df=2; p<.01

The results showed statistical significance for all three categories. Service advertisements were likely to emphasize more on expressive and directive speech acts than durable and non-durable product advertisements. On the other hand, poetic speech acts were emphasized more by durable product ads.

Speech Acts in Advertising (by Type of Magazine, Within Country)

When the variable "speech acts" in advertising within each country was analyzed by type of magazine, the results showed that the use of various speech acts did not differ significantly within each individual country across two magazine categories (news magazine and business magazine).

Table 24 presents the number and percentages of advertisements in two U.S. magazines using various types of speech acts.

Table 24   Speech Acts in Advertising (U.S. Ads by Type of Magazine)

Speech Act	Time	Business Week	
Expressive	45 (60%, n=75)	53 (71%, n=75)	X^2=1.88; df=1; p=.16
Directive	47 (63%, n=75)	44 (59%, n=75)	X^2=.25; df=1; p=.61
Poetic	8 (11%, n=75)	6 (8%, n=75)	X^2=.31; df=1; p=.57

The results indicated that there was no statistically significant difference in the use of speech acts in advertising of the two U.S. magazines.

Table 25 presents the number and percentages of advertisements in two Indian magazines using various types of speech acts.

67

Table 25   Speech Act in Advertising (Indian Ads by Type of Magazine)

Speech Act	India Today	Business India	
Expressive	27 (36%, n=75)	41 (55%, n=75)	X^2=5.27; df=1; p=.02
Directive	35 (47%, n=75)	36 (48%, n=75)	X^2=.02; df=1; p=.87
Poetic	29 (39%, n=75)	20 (27%, n=75)	X^2=2.45; df=1; p=.11

The results indicated that there was no statistically significant difference in the use of speech acts in advertising of the two Indian magazines.

Comparative Approach in Advertising

Comparative Approach (by Country)

The analysis of the variable "comparative approach" revealed that there were differences in the use of comparative approaches in advertisements of the two countries.

Table 26 presents the number and percentages of advertisements using different comparative approaches in the two countries. The results indicated that a greater percentages of the U.S. advertisements utilized explicit and implicit comparative approaches while a greater percentage of Indian ads used unsubstantiated claims. About 3% of the U.S. ads used implicit/indirect comparative technique while this approach was used by only .7% of the Indian advertisements. Also about 1% of the U.S. ads used explicit comparisons while none of the Indian ads utilized this approach. On the other hand, 8% of the Indian ads used puffery/unsubstantiated claims while 2% of the U.S. ads used this approach. Chi-square analysis was not performed because of small size of cells.

68

Table 26   Use of Comparative Approach (by Country)

Use of Comparative Approach	U.S. Ads	Indian Ads
Explicit Comparison	2 (1%, n=150)	0 (n=150)
Implicit Comparison	4 (3%, n=150)	1 (.7%, n=150)
Unsubstantiated Claims	3 (2%, n=150)	12 (8%, n=150)

Comparative Approach (by Type of Product, Between Countries)

The two countries also differed in the use of comparative approaches across different product categories. However, the differences could not be tested for statistical significance with chi-square tests because of small size of cells.

Table 27 presents the number and percentages of durable product advertisements using different comparative approaches in the two countries.

Table 27   Use of Comparative Approach (Durable Product Ads)

Comparative Approach	U.S. Durable	Indian Durable
Explicit Comparison	0 (n=50)	0 (n=50)
Implicit Comparison	0 (n=50)	0 (n=50)
Unsubstantiated Claims	0 (n=50)	5 (10%, n=50)

Table 28 presents the number and percentages of non-durable product advertisements using different comparative approaches in the two countries.

Table 28   Use of Comparative Approach (Non-Durable Product Ads)

Comparative Approach	U.S. Non-Durable	Indian Non-Durable
Explicit Comparison	1 (2%, n=50)	0 (n=50)
Implicit Comparison	0 (n=50)	0 (n=50)
Unsubstantiated Claims	2 (4%, n=50)	3 (6%, n=50)

Table 29 presents the number and percentages of service advertisements using different comparative approaches in the two countries.

Table 29   Use of Comparative Approach (Service Ads)

Comparative Approach	U.S. Durable	Indian Durable
Explicit Comparison	1 (2%, n=50)	0 (n=50)
Implicit Comparison	4 (8%, n=50)	1 (2%, n=50)
Unsubstantiated Claims	1 (2%, n=50)	4 (8%, n=50)

Comparative Approach (by Type of Product, Within Country)

When the variable "comparative approach" in advertising was analyzed by type of product within each country, the results did not show any considerable differences. The minor differences could not be tested for statistical significance with chi-square tests because of small size of cells.

Table 30 presents the number and percentages of U.S. advertisements using different comparative approaches.

Table 30 Use of Comparative Approach (U.S. Ads by Type of Product)

Comparative Approach	Durable	Non- Durable	Service
Explicit Comparison	0 (n=50)	1 (2%, n=50)	1 (2%, n=50)
Implicit Comparison	0 (n=50)	0 (n=50)	4 (8%, n=50)
Unsubstantiated Claims	0 (n=50)	2 (4%, n=50)	1 (2%, n=50)

Table 31 presents the number and percentages of Indian advertisements using different comparative approaches.

Table 31 Use of Comparative Approach (Indian Ads by Type of Product)

Comparative Approach	Durable	Non- Durable	Service
Explicit Comparison	0 (n=50)	0 (n=50)	0 (n=50)
Implicit Comparison	0 (n=50)	0 (n=50)	1 (2%, n=50)
Unsubstantiated Claims	5 (10%, n=50)	3 (6%, n=50)	4 (8%, n=50)

Comparative Approach (by Type of Magazine, Within Country)

When the variable "comparative approach" in advertising within each country was analyzed by type of magazine, the results showed that the use of various comparative approaches did not differ considerably within each individual country across two magazine categories (news magazine and business magazine). The minor differences could not be tested for statistical significance with chi-square tests because of small size of cells.

71

Table 32 presents the number and percentages of advertisements in two U.S. magazines using various types of comparative techniques.

Table 32   Use of Comparative Approach (U.S. Ads by Type of Magazine)

Comparative Approach	Time	Business Week
Explicit	1 (1%, n=75)	1 (1%, n=75)
Implicit	2 (2%, n=75)	2 (2%, n=75)
Unsubstantiated	0 (n=75)	3 (4%, n=75)

Table 33 presents the number and percentages of advertisements in two Indian magazines using various types of comparative approaches.

Table 33   Comparative Approach (Indian Ads by Type of Magazine)

Comparative Approach	India Today	Business India
Explicit	0 (n=75)	0 (n=75)
Implicit	0 (n=75)	1 (1%, n=75)
Unsubstantiated	7 (9%, n=75)	5 (6%, n=75)

Iconic Stance of Human Characters in Advertising

Iconic Stance of Human Characters (by Country)

The analysis of the variable "iconic image of human character" revealed that there were significant differences in advertisements of the two countries.

Table 34 presents the number and percentages of advertisements using individualistic and collective stance within the two countries. The results indicate that 86% of the U.S. advertisements (featuring human characters) used individualistic stance while this approach was used by 53% of the Indian advertisements. On the other hand, 47% of the Indian ads used collective stance while only 14% of the U.S. ads used this approach. A chi-square analysis

72

showed that the differences were statistically significant ($X^2=34.04$, df=1, p<.001). Therefore, it is concluded that U.S. ads are more likely to use individualistic stance, and Indian ads tend to favor collective stance for human characters.

Table 34   Iconic Stance of Human Characters (by Country)

Iconic Image	U.S. Ads	Indian Ads
Individualistic Stance	117 (86%, n=136)	68 (53%, n=128)
Collective Stance	19 (14%, n=136)	60 (47%, n=128)

Chi-square=34.04;   d.f.=1;   p<.001

Iconic Stance of Human Characters (by Type of Product, Between Countries)

The two countries also differed in the use of individualistic and collective stance across different product categories. When the variable "iconic stance of human character" in advertising between the two countries was analyzed by type of product, the results showed statistically significant differences for all three product categories.

Table 35 presents the number and percentages of durable product advertisements using individualistic and collective stance in the two countries. The analysis revealed that the tendency that was found for the use of individualistic and collective stance between the two countries (regardless of type of product) also held across durable product ad category. The results indicate that 83% of the U.S. durable product (featuring human characters) advertisements used individualistic stance while this approach was used by only 52% of the Indian durable product advertisements. On the other hand, 48% of the Indian ads used collective stance while only 17% of the U.S. ads used this approach. A chi-square analysis showed that the differences were statistically significant ($X^2=9.69$, df=1, p=.001). Therefore, it is concluded that U.S. ads are more likely to use individualistic stance, and Indian ads tend to favor collective stance for human characters.

73

Table 35   Iconic Stance of Human Characters (Durable Product Ads)

Iconic Image	U.S. Ads	Indian Ads
Individualistic Stance	38 (83%, n=46)	24 (52%, n=46)
Collective Stance	8 (17%, n=46)	22 (48%, n=46)

X^2=9.69, df=1, p=.001

Table 36 presents the number and percentages of non-durable advertisements using individualistic and collective stance in the two countries. The analysis revealed that the tendency that was found for the use of individualistic and collective stance between the two countries (regardless of type of product) also held across non-durable product ad category.

The results indicate that 94% of the U.S. non-durable product advertisements (featuring human characters) used individualistic stance while this approach was used by 59% of the Indian non-durable product advertisements. On the other hand, 41% of the Indian ads used collective stance while only 6% of the U.S. ads used this approach. A chi-square analysis showed that the differences were statistically significant (X^2=14.86, df=1, p<.001).

Table 36 Iconic Stance of Human Characters (Non-Durable Ads)

Iconic Image	U.S. Ads	Indian Ads
Individualistic Stance	44 (94%, n=47)	23 (59%, n=39)
Collective Stance	3 (6%, n=47)	16 (41%, n=39)

X^2=14.86, df=1, p<.001

Table 37 presents the number and percentages of service advertisements using individualistic and collective stance within the two countries. The analysis revealed that the tendency that was found for the use of individualistic and collective stance between the two countries (regardless of type of product) also held across service ad category. The results indicate that 81% of the U.S. service advertisements (featuring human characters) used individualistic stance while this approach was used by 49% of Indian advertisements. On the other hand, 51% of the Indian ads used collective stance while only 19% of the U.S. ads used this approach. A chi-square analysis showed that the differences were statistically significant.

Table 37   Iconic Stance of Human Characters (Service Ads)

Iconic Image	U.S. Ads	Indian Ads
Individualistic Stance	35 (81%, n=43)	21 (49%, n=43)
Collective Stance	8 (19%, n=43)	22 (51%, n=43)

X^2=10.03, df=1, p=.001

Iconic Stance of Human Characters (by Type of Product, Within Country)

When the variable "iconic stance of human characters" in advertising within each country was analyzed by type of product, the results did not show any statistically significant difference.

Table 38 presents the number and percentages of U.S. durable, non-durable and service advertisements using individualistic and collective visual stance for human characters.

Table 38   Iconic Stance of Characters (U.S. Ads by Type of Product)

Iconic Image	Durable	Non-Durable	Service
Individualistic	38 (83%, n=46)	44 (94%, n=47)	35 (81%, n=43)
Collective	8 (17%, n=46)	3 (6%, n=47)	8 (19%, n=43)

X^2=3.46; df=2; p=.17

75

Table 39 presents the number and percentages of U.S. durable, non-durable and service advertisements using individualistic and collective visual stance for human characters.

Table 39   Iconic Stance of Characters (Indian Ads by Type of Product)

Iconic Image	Durable	Non-Durable	Service
Individualistic	24 (52%, n=46)	23 (59%, n=39)	21 (49%, n=43)
Collective	22 (48%, n=46)	16 (41%, n=39)	22 (51%, n=43)

X^2=.87; df=2; p=.64

Iconic Stance of Human Characters (by Type of Magazine, Within Country)

When the variable "iconic stance of human characters" in advertising within each country was analyzed by type of magazine, the results showed that the use of the two visual stances did not differ significantly within each individual country across two magazine categories (news magazine and business magazine).

Table 40 presents the number and percentages of advertisements in two U.S. magazines using various types of visual stance.

Table 40   Iconic Stance of Characters (U.S. Ads by Type of Magazine)

Iconic Image	Time	Business Week
Individualistic	62 (93%, n=67)	55 (80%, n=69)
Collective	5 (7%, n=67)	14 (20%, n=69)

X^2=4.65; df=1; p=.03

The results indicated that there was no statistically significant difference in the use of two visual stances in advertising of the two U.S. magazines.

Table 41 presents the number and percentages of advertisements in two Indian magazines using various types of visual stance.

Table 41   Iconic Stance of Characters   (Indian Ads by Type of Magazine)

Iconic Image	India Today	Business India
Individualistic	35 (54%, n=65)	33 (52%, n=63)
Collective	30 (46%, n=65)	30 (48%, n=63)

X^2=6.76; df=2; p=.03

The results indicated that there was no statistically significant difference in the use of two visual stances in advertising of the two Indian magazines.

Indexical Feature Transfer in Advertising

Indexical Feature Transfer (by Country)

The analysis of the variable "indexical feature transfer" revealed that there were some differences in advertisements of the two countries. However, these differences were found to be statistically nonsignificant. Table 42 presents the number and percentages of advertisements using different indexical feature transfer approaches in the two countries. The results indicate that about 5% of the U.S. ads used "physical attractiveness attribute" while this approach was used by 4% of the Indian advertisements. About 17% of the U.S. ads used "loving caring attribute" while 18% of the Indian ads utilized this approach. On the other hand, comparatively a larger percentage of the Indian ads (5%) used "status attribute" while only .7% of the U.S. ads used this approach. A chi-square analysis showed that the differences were not statistically significant (X^2=4.86, df=3, p=.18). Therefore, it is concluded that the use of these three indexical feature transfer techniques are similar in the two countries.

77

Table 42   Indexical Feature Transfer (by Country)

Indexical Feature Transfer	U.S. Ads	Indian Ads
Physical Attractiveness	7 (5%, n=150)	6 (4%, n=150)
Status Attribute	1 (.7%, n=150)	7 (5%, n=150)
Loving Caring Attribute	25 (17%, n=150)	27(18%, n=150)

X^2=4.86, df=2, p=.18

Indexical Feature Transfer (by Type of Product, Between Countries)

The two countries also exhibited similarities in the use of "indexical feature transfer" in advertising across different types of product. Minor differences were not tested with chi-square tests because of small size of cells.

Table 43 presents the number and percentages of durable product advertisements using different indexical feature transfer approaches in the two countries.

Table 43   Indexical Feature Transfer (Durable Product Ads)

Indexical Feature Transfer	U.S. Ads	Indian Ads
Physical Attractiveness	2 (4%, n=50)	2 (4%, n=50)
Status Attribute	1 (2%, n=50)	3 (6%, n=50)
Loving Caring Attribute	3 (6%, n=50)	5 (10%, n=50)

Table 44 presents the number and percentages of non-durable product advertisements using different indexical feature transfer approaches within the two countries.

Table 44   Indexical Feature Transfer (Non-Durable Product Ads)

Indexical Feature Transfer	U.S. Ads	Indian Ads
Physical Attractiveness	4 (8%, n=50)	3 (6%, n=50)
Status Attribute	0 (n=50)	2 (4%, n=50)
Loving Caring Attribute	11 (22%, n=50)	9 (18%, n=50)

Table 45 presents the number and percentages of service ads using different indexical feature transfer approaches within the two countries.

Table 45   Indexical Feature Transfer (Service Ads)

Indexical Feature Transfer	U.S. Ads	Indian Ads
Physical Attractiveness	1 (2%, n=50)	1 (2%, n=50)
Status Attribute	0 (n=50)	2 (4%, n=50)
Loving Caring Attribute	11 (22%, n=50)	13 (26%, n=50)

Indexical Feature Transfer (by Type of Product, Within Country)

When the variable "indexical feature transfer" in advertising within each country was analyzed by type of product, the results indicated that the use of the three indexical feature transfer techniques did not vary considerably across durable product, non-durable product and service advertisements. Minor differences were not tested with chi-square tests because of small size of cells.

Table 46 presents the number and percentages of U.S. advertisements using different indexical transfer approaches.

Table 46   Indexical Feature Transfer (U.S. Ads by Type of Product)

Indexical Feature Transfer	Durable	Non- Durable	Service
Physical Attractiveness	2 (4%, n=50)	4 (8%, n=50)	1 (2%, n=50)
Status Attribute	1 (2%, n=50)	0 (n=50)	0 (n=50)
Loving caring Attribute	3 (6%, n=50)	11 (22%, n=50)	11 (22%, n=50)

Table 47 presents the number and percentages of Indian advertisements using different indexical transfer approaches.

Table 47 Indexical Feature Transfer (Indian Ads by Type of Product)

Indexical Feature Transfer	Durable	Non- Durable	Service
Physical Attractiveness	2 (4%, n=50)	3 (6%, n=50)	1 (2%, n=50)
Status Attribute	3 (6%, n=50)	2 (4%, n=50)	2 (4%, n=50)
Loving Caring Attribute	5 (10%, n=50)	9 (18%, n=50)	13 (26%, n=50)

Indexical Feature Transfer (by Type of Magazine, Within Country)

When the variable "indexical feature transfer" in advertising within each country was analyzed by type of magazine, the results showed that the use of the three indexical feature transfer approaches did not differ considerably within each individual country across two magazine categories (news magazine and business magazine). Minor differences were not tested with chi-square tests because of small size of cells.

80

Table 48 presents the number and percentages of advertisements in two U.S. magazines using various types of indexical feature transfer approaches.

Table 48   Indexical Feature Transfer (U.S. Ads by Type of Magazine)

Indexical Feature	Time	Business Week
Physical Attractiveness	7 (9%, n=75)	0 (n=75)
Status Attribute	0 (n=75)	1 (1%, n=75)
Loving/Caring	17 (23%, n=75)	8 (11%, n=50)

Table 49 presents the number and percentages of advertisements in two Indian magazines using various types of indexical feature transfer approaches.

Table 49   Indexical Feature Transfer (Indian Ads by Type of Magazine)

Indexical Feature	India Today	Business India
Physical Attractiveness	5 (6%, n=75)	1 (1%, n=75)
Status Attribute	4 (5%, n=75)	3 (4%, n=75)
Loving/Caring	15 (20%, n=75)	12 (16%, n=75)

Iconic Image of Women in Advertising

Iconic Image of Women (by Country)

The analysis of the variable "iconic image of women" revealed that there were significant differences in the way advertisements of the two countries portrayed women.

Table 50 presents the number and percentages of advertisements containing different types of portrayals of women within the two countries. The results indicate that a greater percentage of Indian ads contained stereotypical images of women. Among the ads that had women characters, about 54% of Indian ads were somewhat stereotypical as compared to 29% of

81

the U.S. ads. Also, about 16% of the Indian ads were highly stereotypical compared to only 5% of the U.S. advertisements. A chi-square analysis showed that the differences were statistically significant (X^2=23.03, df=4, p<.001). A t test of the mean scores also confirms statistical significance (Table 51).

Table 50   Stereotypical Image of Women (by Country)

Stereotypical Image of Women	U.S. Ads	Indian Ads
Highly Stereotypical	3 (5%, n=63)	14 (16%, n=88)
Somewhat Stereotypical	18 (29%, n=63)	47 (54%, n=88)
Neutral	33 (52%, n=63)	23 (26%, n=88)
Somewhat Non-stereotypical	2 (3%, n=63)	3 (3.4%, n=88)
Entirely Non-stereotypical	7 (11%, n=63)	1 (1.1%, n=88)

Chi-square=23.03;   d.f.=4;   p<.001

Table 51 Mean Scores For Stereotypical Image of Women (by Country)

Country	Mean	
U.S.	3.13	(n=63)
Indian	3.80	(n=88)

t=-4.64; df= 149; p<.001

Table 52 presents the number and percentages of advertisements showing different levels of physical exploitation of women within the two countries. The results indicate that a greater percentage of U.S. ads used physical exploitation of women and portrayed women as sex objects.

Among the ads that had women characters, about 13% of the U.S. ads had very high physical exploitation as compared to only 2% for the Indian ads. Also, about 13% of the U.S. ads had moderate exploitation compared to only 4.5% for the Indian advertisements. A larger percentage of Indian ads (89%) had no physical exploitation compared to 74% for the U.S. advertisements.

A chi-square analysis showed that the differences were statistically significant (X^2=12.83, df=3, p<.01). A t test of the mean scores also confirms statistical significance (Table 53).

Table 52   Portrayals of Women as Sex Objects (by Country)

Women as Sex Objects	U.S. Ads	Indian Ads
Very High Exploitation	8 (13%, n=63)	2 (2%, n=88)
Moderate Exploitation	8 (13%, n=63)	4 (4.5%, n=88)
No Exploitation	47 (74%, n=63)	78 (89%, n=88)

Chi-square=12.83;   d.f.=4;   p<.01

Table 53 Mean Scores for Portrayals of Women as Sex Objects (by Country)

Country	Mean	
U.S.	1.76	(n=63)
Indian	1.23	(n=88)

t=3.02; df=149; p<.01

Iconic Image of Women (by Type of Product, Between Countries)

The two countries also differed in the portrayal of women across several product categories. When the variable "iconic image of women" in advertising between the two countries was analyzed by type of product, the results showed statistically significant differences for several categories.

Table 54 presents the mean scores for stereotypical image of women in durable product ads of the two countries. It reveals that the Indian durable ads had higher mean score than their U.S. counterparts. A t test of the mean scores confirms statistical significance. Therefore, it is concluded that the Indian durable product ads were more likely to contain stereotypical images of women.

Table 54 Mean Scores For Stereotypical Image (Durable Ads)

Country	Mean	
U.S.	3.22	(n=23)
Indian	3.97	(n=34)

t=-3.24; df=55; p<.01

Table 55 presents the mean scores for portrayal of women as sex objects in durable product ads of the two countries. It reveals that the U.S. durable product ads had slightly higher mean score than their Indian counterparts. A t test of the mean scores, however, did not show any statistical significance.

Table 55 Mean Scores for Portrayals of Women as Sex Objects (Durable Ads)

Country	Mean	
U.S.	1.43	(n=23)
Indian	1.29	(n=34)

t=.57; df=55; p=.57

Table 56 presents the mean scores for stereotypical image of women in non-durable product ads of the two countries. It reveals that the Indian non-durable ads had higher mean score than their U.S. counterparts. A t test of the mean scores confirms statistical significance. Therefore, it is concluded that the Indian non-durable product ads were more likely to contain stereotypical images of women.

Table 56 Mean Scores for Stereotypical Image (Non-Durable Ads)

Country	Mean	
U.S.	2.95	(n=22)
Indian	3.84	(n=25)

t=-3.57; df=45; p=.001

Table 57 presents the mean scores for portrayal of women as sex objects in non-durable product ads of the two countries. It reveals that the U.S. non-durable product ads had slightly higher mean score than their Indian counterparts. A t test of the mean scores, however, did not show any statistical significance.

Table 57 Mean Scores for Portrayals of Women as Sex Objects (Non-Durable)

Country	Mean	
U.S.	2.00	(n=22)
Indian	1.36	(n=25)

t=1.69; df=45; p=.09

Table 58 presents the mean scores for stereotypical image of women in service ads of the two countries. It reveals that Indian service ads had slightly higher mean score than their U.S. counterparts. A t test of the mean scores, however, did not show any statistical significance.

Table 58 Mean Scores for Stereotypical Image of Women (Service Ads)

Country	Mean	
U.S.	3.22	(n=18)
Indian	3.55	(n=29)

t=-1.22; df=45; p=.22

Table 59 presents the mean scores for portrayal of women as sex objects in service ads of the two countries. It reveals that the U.S. service ads had slightly higher mean score than their Indian counterparts. A t test of the mean scores confirms statistical significance.

Table 59 Mean Scores for Portrayals of Women as Sex Objects (Service Ads)

Country	Mean	
U.S.	1.89	(n=18)
Indian	1.03	(n=29)

t=2.92; df=45; p<.01

Iconic Image of Women (by Type of Product, Within Country)

When the variable "iconic image of women" in advertising was analyzed within each country by type of product, the results did not find any differences which were statistically significant.

Table 60 presents the mean scores for stereotypical image of women in durable, non-durable and service ads of the United States. An ANOVA test shows that there was no statistically significant difference among the ads across different product categories.

Table 60 Mean Scores for Stereotypical Image (U.S. Ads by Product)

Type of Product	Mean	
Durable Product Ads	3.22	(n=23)
Non-Durable Product Ads	2.95	(n=22)
Service Ads	3.22	(n=18)

F=.520; df=2, 62; p=.59

Table 61 presents the mean scores for portrayal of women as sex objects in durable, non-durable and service ads of the United States. An ANOVA test shows that there was no statistically significant difference among the ads across different product categories.

Table 61 Mean Scores for Portrayals as Sex Objects (U.S. Ads by Product)

Type of Product	Mean	
Durable Product Ads	1.43	(n=23)
Non-Durable Product Ads	2.00	(n=22)
Service Ads	1.89	(n=18)

F=.1.00; df=2, 62; p=.37

87

Table 62 presents the mean scores for stereotypical image of women in durable, non-durable and service ads of India. An ANOVA test shows that there was no statistically significant difference among the ads across different product categories.

Table 62 Mean Scores for Stereotypical Image (Indian Ads by Product)

Type of Product	Mean	
Durable Product Ads	3.97	(n=34)
Non-Durable Product Ads	3.84	(n=25)
Service Ads	3.55	(n=29)

F=2.32; df=2, 87; p=.10

Table 63 presents the mean scores for portrayal of women as sex objects in durable, non-durable and service ads of India. An ANOVA test shows that there was no statistically significant difference among the ads across different product categories.

Table 63 Means for Portrayals as Sex Objects (Indian Ads by Product)

Type of Product	Mean	
Durable Product Ads	1.29	(n=34)
Non-Durable Product Ads	1.36	(n=25)
Service Ads	1.03	(n=29)

F=1.55; df=2, 87; p=.21

Iconic Image of Women (by Type of Magazine, Within Country)

When the variable "iconic image of women" in advertising was analyzed within each country by type of magazine, the results did not find any differences which were statistically significant.

88

Table 64 presents the mean scores for stereotypical image of women in advertisements of the U.S. magazines. A t test shows that there was no statistically significant difference between the ads of the two magazines.

Table 64 Mean Scores for Stereotypical Image (U.S. Ads by Magazine)

Type of Magazine	Mean	
Time	3.24	(n=41)
Business Week	2.91	(n=22)

t=1.31; df=61; p=.19

Table 65 presents the mean scores for portrayal of women as sex objects in advertisements of the U.S. magazines. A t test shows that there was no statistically significant difference between the ads of the two magazines.

Table 65 Means for Portrayals as Sex Objects (U.S. Ads by Magazine)

Type of Magazine	Mean	
Time	1.93	(n=41)
Business Week	1.45	(n=22)

t=1.27; df=61; p=.20

Table 66 presents the mean scores for stereotypical image of women in advertisements of the Indian magazines. A t test shows that there was no statistically significant difference between the ads of the two magazines.

Table 66 Means for Stereotypical Image (Indian Ads by Magazine)

Type of Magazine	Mean	
India Today	3.73	(n=48)
Business India	3.88	(n=40)

t=-.86; df=86; p=.39

Table 67 presents the mean scores for portrayal of women as sex objects in advertisements of the Indian magazines. A t test shows that there was no statistically significant difference between the ads of the two magazines.

Table 67 Means for Portrayals as Sex Objects (Indian Ads by Magazine)

Type of Magazine	Mean	
India Today	1.23	(n=48)
Business India	1.23	(n=40)

t=.03; df=86; p=.97

Demographic Variables

Demographic Variables (by Country)

The advertisements of the two countries were also analyzed in terms of several demographic variables. The results found significant differences between the two countries in the use of male and female characters in advertising.

Gender of Human Characters. Table 68 presents the number and percentages of advertisements featuring male and female characters within the two countries. The results indicate that a greater percentage of the U.S. ads featured male characters alone. Among the ads that had human characters, about 47% of the U.S. ads featured male characters alone compared to 25% for the female characters. On the other hand, about 26% of the Indian ads featured male characters alone compared to about 19% female characters alone. A chi-square analysis showed that the differences were statistically significant (X^2=21.97, df=2, p<.001).

Table 68   Gender of Human Characters (by Country)

Gender of Human Characters	U.S. Ads	Indian Ads
Male Only	64 (47%, n=136)	33 (25.6%, n=129)
Female Only	34 (25%, n=136)	24 (18.6%, n=129)
Neutral	38 (28%, n=136)	72 (55.8%, n=129)

Chi-square=21.97;   d.f.=2;   p<.001

Use of Children, Elderly, Cartoons, Animals (by Country).Table 69 presents the number and percentages of advertisements featuring children, elderly, cartoons and animals. Although there are some differences in the use of three of the variables (elderly, cartoons. animals), chi-square analysis indicated that these differences were not statistically significant.

Table 69 Use of Children, Elderly, Cartoons, Animals (by Country)

Variable	U.S. Ads	Indian Ads	
Children	33 (22%, n=150)	33 (22%, n=150)	X^2=.00; d.f.=1; p=1.00
Elderly	21 (15%, n=136)	8 (6%, n=129)	X^2=5.79; d.f.=1; p=.01
Cartoons	14 (9%, n=150)	21 (14%, n=150)	X^2=1.58; d.f.=1; p=.20
Animals	10 (7%, n=149)	18 (12%, n=150)	X^2=2.46; d.f.=1; p=.11

Demographic Variables (by Type of Product, Between Countries)

When the demographic variables were analyzed by type of product, the results showed statistically significant difference for several variables.

91

Gender of Human Characters (Durable Product Ads). Table 70 presents the number and percentages of durable product advertisements featuring male and female characters in the two countries. The results indicate that a greater percentage of the U.S. ads featured male characters alone. Among the ads that had human characters, about 39% of the U.S. ads featured male characters alone compared to 28% for the female characters. On the other hand, about 24% of the Indian ads featured male characters alone compared to 17% for the female characters. A chi-square analysis showed that the differences were statistically significant (X^2=6.30, df=2, p<.05).

Table 70   Gender of Human Characters (Durable Product Ads)

Gender of Human Characters	U.S. Ads	Indian Ads
Male Only	18 (39%, n=46)	11 (24%, n=46)
Female Only	13 (28%, n=46)	8 (17%, n=46)
Neutral	15 (33%, n=46)	27 (59%, n=46)

Chi Square=6.30;   d.f.=2;   p<.01

Use of Children, Elderly, Cartoons, Animals (Durable Ads). Table 71 presents the number and percentages of durable product advertisements featuring children, elderly, cartoons and animals. Although there are some differences in the use of two of the variables (children, animals), chi-square analysis indicated that these differences were not statistically significant.

Table 71   Use of Children, Elderly, Cartoons, Animals (Durable Ads)

Variable	U.S. Ads	Indian Ads	
Children	10 (20%, n=50)	9 (18%, n=50)	X^2=.06; d.f.=1; p=.79
Animals	5 (10%, n=50)	2 (4%, n=50)	X^2=1.38; d.f.=1; p=.23
Elderly	3 (7%, n=46)	4 (9%, n=46)	cell size inadequate
Cartoons	4 (8%, n=50)	4 (8%, n=50)	cell size inadequate

Gender of Human Characters (Non-Durable Product Ads). Table 72 presents the number and percentages of non-durable product advertisements featuring male and female characters in the two countries. The results indicate that a greater percentage of the U.S. ads featured male characters alone, while a greater percentage of the Indian ads featured both male and female characters. Among the ads that had human characters, about 53% of the U.S. ads featured male characters alone compared to 30% for the female characters. On the other hand, about 32% of the Indian ads featured male characters alone compared to 17% for the female characters. A chi-square analysis showed that the differences were statistically significant (X^2=11.59, df=2, p<.01).

Table 72   Gender of Human Characters (Non-Durable Product Ads)

Gender of Human Characters	U.S. Ads	Indian Ads
Male Only	25 (53%, n=47)	13 (32%, n=41)
Female Only	14 (30%, n=47)	7 (17%, n=41)
Neutral	8 (17%, n=47)	21 (51%, n=41)

X^2=11.59, df=2, p<.01

Use of Children, Elderly, Cartoons, Animals (Non-Durable Ads). Table 73 presents the number and percentages of non-durable product ads featuring children, elderly, cartoons and animals. Although there are some differences in the use of these variables (children, elderly, cartoons, animals), chi-square analysis showed significant difference between the two countries for only one variable "presence of elderly character." The results indicated that a greater percentage of U.S. non-durable product ads featured elderly characters than their Indian counterparts.

93

Table 73 Use of Children, Elderly, Cartoons, Animals (Non-Durable Ads)

Variable	U.S. Ads	Indian Ads	
Children	6 (12%, n=50)	7 (14%, n=50)	X^2=.08; d.f.=1; p=.76
Elderly	10 (21%, n=47)	1 (2%, n=41)	X^2=7.10; d.f.=1; p<.01
Cartoons	3 (6%, n=50)	9 (18%, n=50)	X^2=3.40; d.f.=1; p=.06
Animals	3 (6%, n=50)	7 (14%, n=50)	X^2=1.77; d.f.=1; p=.18

Gender of Human Characters (Service Ads). Table 74 presents the number and percentages of service advertisements featuring male and female characters in the two countries. The results indicate that a greater percentage of the U.S. ads featured male characters alone, while a greater percentage of the Indian ads featured both male and female characters. Among the ads that had human characters, about 49% of the U.S. ads featured male characters alone compared to only 16% for the female characters. On the other hand, about 21% of the Indian ads featured male characters alone. About same percentage (21%) of the Indian ads also featured female characters alone. A chi-square analysis showed that the differences were statistically significant.

Table 74   Gender of Human Characters (Service Ads)

Gender of Human Characters	U.S. Ads	Indian Ads
Male Only	21 (49%, n=43)	9 (21.4%, n=42)
Female Only	7 (16%, n=43)	9 (21.4%, n=42)
Neutral	15 (35%, n=43)	24 (57.2%, n=42)

X^2=7.11, df=2, p=.02

Use of Children, Elderly, Cartoons, Animals (Service Ads). Table 75 presents the number and percentages of service advertisements featuring children, elderly, cartoons and animals.

Although there are some differences in the use of three of the variables (elderly, cartoons, animals), chi-square analysis did not show any statistical significance.

Table 75   Use of Children, Elderly, Cartoons, Animals (Service Ads)

Variable	U.S. Ads	Indian Ads	
Children	17 (34%, n=50)	17 (34%, n=50)	X^2=.00; d.f.=1; p=1.00
Elderly	8 (19%, n=43)	3 (7%, n=42)	X^2=2.47; d.f.=1; p=.11
Cartoons	7 (14%, n=50)	8 (16%, n=50)	X^2=.07; d.f.=1; p=.77
Animals	2 (4%, n=49)	9 (18%, n=50)	X^2=4.85; d.f.=1; p=.02

Demographic Variables (by Type of Product, Within Country)

When the demographic variables were analyzed by type of product within each country, the results showed no statistically significant differences.

Gender of Human Characters (U.S. Ads). Table 76 presents the number and percentages of U.S. durable product, non-durable product and service advertisements featuring male and female characters. Although there were minor differences, a chi-square analysis indicated that they were statistically nonsignificant.

Table 76 Gender of Human Characters (U.S. Ads by Type of Product)

Gender	Durable	Non-durable	Service
Male Only	18 (39%, n=46)	25 (53%, n=47)	21 (49%, n=43)
Female Only	13 (28%, n=46)	14 (30%, n=47)	7 (16%, n=43)
Neutral	15 (33%, n=46)	8 (17%, n=47)	15 (35%, n=43)

Chi-square=6.05;   d.f.=4;   p=.19

Use of Children, Elderly, Cartoons, Animals (U.S. Ads). Table 77 presents the number and percentages of U.S. durable product, non-durable product and service advertisements featuring children, elderly, cartoons and animals. Although there are some differences in the use of these variables, chi-square analysis showed no statistical significance.

Table 77 Children, Elderly, Cartoons, Animals (U.S. Ads by Product)

Variable	Durable	Non-durable	Service	
Children	10 (20%, n=50)	6 (12%, n=50)	17 (34%, n=50)	X^2=7.22, df=2, p=.02
Elderly	3 (7%, n=46)	10 (21%, n=47)	8 (19%, n=43)	X^2=4.35, df=2, p=.11
Cartoons	4 (8%, n=50)	3 (6%, n=50)	7 (14%, n=50)	X^2=2.04, df=2, p=.35
Animals	5 (10%, n=50)	3 (6%, n=50)	2 (4%, n=50)	X^2=1.44, df=2, p=.48

Gender of Human Characters (Indian Ads). Table 78 presents the number and percentages of Indian durable product, non-durable product and service advertisements featuring male and female characters. Although there were minor differences, a chi-square analysis indicated that they were statistically non-significant.

Table 78 Gender of Human Characters (Indian Ads by Type of Product)

Gender	Durable	Non-durable	Service
Male Only	11 (24%, n=46)	13 (32%, n=41)	9 (21.4%, n=42)
Female Only	8 (17%, n=46)	7 (17%, n=41)	9 (21.4%, n=42)
Neutral	27 (59%, n=46)	21 (51%, n=41)	24 (57.2%, n=42)

Chi-square=1.43;   d.f.=4;   p=.83

Use of Children, Elderly, Cartoons, Animals (Indian Ads). Table 79 presents the number and percentages of Indian durable product, non-durable product and service advertisements

featuring children, elderly, cartoons and animals. Although there are some differences in the use
of these variables, chi square analyses showed no statistical significance.

Table 79 Children, Elderly, Cartoons, Animals (Indian Ads by Product)

Variable	Durable	Non-durable	Service	
Cartoons	4 (8%, n=50)	9 (18%, n=50)	8 (16%, n=50)	X^2=2.32, df=2, p=.31
Animals	2 (4%, n=50)	7 (14%, n=50)	9 (18%, n=50)	X^2=4.92, df=2, p=.08
Children	9 (18%, n=50)	7 (14%, n=50)	17 (34%, n=50)	X^2=6.52, df=2, p=.03
Elderly	4 (9%, n=46)	1 (2%, n=41)	3 (7%, n=42)	Inadequate Cell Size

Demographic Variables (by Type of Magazine, Within Country)

When the demographic variables were analyzed by type of magazine within each country,
the results showed no statistically significant differences.

Gender of Human Characters (U.S. Ads). Table 80 presents the number and percentages
advertisements in the two U.S. magazines featuring male and female characters. A chi-square
analysis indicated that there were no statistically significant differences.

Table 80 Gender of Human Characters (U.S. Ads by Type of Magazine)

Gender	Time	Business Week
Male Only	23 (34%, n=67)	41 (59.4%, n=69)
Female Only	22 (33%, n=67)	12 (17.4%, n=69)
Neutral	22 (33%, n=67)	16 (23.2%, n=69)

Chi-square=8.92; d.f.=2; p=.01

Use of Children, Elderly, Cartoons, Animals (U.S. Ads). Table 81 presents the number and percentages of advertisements in the two U.S. magazines featuring children, elderly, cartoons and animals. Chi-square analysis showed no statistical significance for any of the variables.

Table 81 Children, Elderly, Cartoons, Animals (U.S. Ads by Magazine)

Variable	Time	Business Week	
Cartoons	8 (11%, n=75)	6 (8%, n=75)	$X^2=.31$, df=1, p=.57
Animals	5 (6%, n=75)	5 (6%, n=75)	$X^2=.00$, df=1, p=.98
Children	17 (23%, n=75)	16 (21%, n=75)	$X^2=.03$, df=1, p=.84
Elderly	8 (12%, n=75)	13 (19%, n=75)	$X^2=1.23$, df=1, p=.26

Gender of Human Characters (Indian Ads). Table 82 presents the number and percentages of advertisements in the two Indian magazines featuring male and female characters. A chi-square analysis indicated that there were no statistically significant differences.

Table 82 Gender of Human Characters (Indian Ads by Magazine)

Gender	India Today	Business India
Male Only	15 (23.4%, n=64)	18 (28%, n=65)
Female Only	13 (20.3%, n=64)	11 (17%, n=65)
Neutral	36 (56.3%, n=64)	36 (55%, n=65)

Chi-square=.43;   d.f.=2;   p=.80

Use of Children, Elderly, Cartoons, Animals (Indian Ads). Table 83 presents the number and percentages of advertisements in the two Indian magazines featuring children, elderly, cartoons and animals. Chi-square analysis showed no statistical significance for any of the variables.

98

Table 83 Children, Elderly, Cartoons, Animals (Indian Ad by Magazine)

Variable	India Today	Business India	
Cartoons	11 (15%, n=75)	10 (13%, n=75)	X^2=.05, df=1, p=.81
Animals	9 (12%, n=75)	9 (12%, n=75)	X^2=.00, df=1, p=1.00
Children	17 (23%, n=75)	16 (21%, n=75)	X^2=.03, df=1, p=.84
Elderly	2 (3%, n=75)	6 (9%, n=75)	X^2=2.06, df=1, p=.15

CHAPTER VI

CONCLUSION

The purpose of this study was to conduct a cross-cultural analysis of the verbal as well as visual content of print advertising from India and the United States to examine the characteristics, differences and similarities in advertising expressions.

To answer the first research question, what are the specific linguistic and visual characteristics of magazine advertisements in the United States and India?, nominal level data measurements such as frequency counts and valid percentages were used for all but two variables. Interval level data measurements such as calculations of means were used for (a) total number of information cues used, and (b) images of women.

To answer the second research question, how do magazine advertisements in the United States and India differ in terms of linguistic codification, visual codification and combined verbal/visual codification?, four types of statistical tests were performed. To test if the variables (generating nominal level data) are significantly different between Indian and U.S. advertising campaigns, chi-square tests and Spearman's rho tests were performed. To test if the variables (generating interval level data) are significantly different, t test and ANOVA tests were performed.

The data analysis revealed that there were significant differences in many aspects of advertising strategies and expressions in India and the United States. The findings also indicated that there are similarities in some aspects of advertising expressions in the two countries.

In the use of information cues, the two countries differed across several categories. Indian advertisements used "availability" information cue more often than did the U.S. advertisements. This tendency also held across durable product, non-durable product and service ads between the two countries. Company sponsored research information cue was found to be used more frequently in the U.S. ads than in Indian advertisements.

100

A significant difference was found between the two countries in durable product ads in terms of "price/value" information cue. The analysis revealed that price/value information cue was more utilized by U.S. durable ads than their Indian counterparts. In both U.S. and Indian ads, "quality/performance" information was the most commonly used cue. In U.S. ads, the second most frequently used information cue was components/ingredients, while in Indian ads, the second most common information cue was availability information. This tendency also held across durable product, non-durable product and service ads between the two countries.

Among the similarities between the two countries in the use of information cues were the mean number of information cues and similar emphasis given to certain cues such as quality-performance, safety, special offers, new ideas, packaging, nutrition, warranties and taste information. The mean number of cues was found to be similar between the two cultures when compared by country regardless of type of product. However, when analyzed across product categories, Indian service ads had a higher mean number of cues. This was due to the fact that Indian service ads made greater use of availability information cues which brought the mean number of cues higher than the U.S. ads. The use of availability information cue was very high for the Indian ads because Indian consumers need to know specific details about where and when the product or service is available.

When information content of advertising was analyzed within each country by type of product, the results revealed that the use of most information cues did not vary within each individual country across product categories, thus supporting the contention that the significant differences that were found between the two countries would hold regardless of product type if differences were also found between countries across different product categories. The U.S. durable product, non-durable product and service advertisements were similar in terms of mean number of information cues. Within the U.S. ads, the only differences were that durable product ads were likely to emphasize more on component information cue than non-durable product and service advertisements. Indian durable product, non-durable product and service advertisements were also similar in terms of mean number of information cues. Within the Indian ads, the only differences were that the durable and service advertisements were likely to emphasize more on quality information cue than non-durable product advertisements.

In the use of speech acts, the two countries differed in all three categories. The results revealed that the U.S. ads used both expressive and directive speech acts more often than did the Indian ads. Conversely, Indian ads utilized poetic speech acts more frequently than did the U.S. ads. These results support the notion that differences in the cultural contexts of the two countries (India being high-context and U.S. being low-context) are reflected in the use of different speech acts. These findings are in agreement with those of other researchers which indicated that advertising in high-context cultures use poetic speech acts more often and advertising in low-context cultures tend to use expressive and directive speech acts more frequently. The two countries also differed in the use of speech acts across different product categories. The results revealed that the tendency that was found for the use of speech acts between the two countries (regardless of type of product) also held across the durable product category. In non-durable product ads, the two countries differed in the use of poetic speech acts. Indian non-durable product ads used poetic speech acts more often than did the U.S. ads. No statistically significant difference was found for the use of expressive and directive speech acts in non-durable ads of the two countries. In service ads, the two countries differed in the use of expressive speech acts. The U.S. service ads used expressive speech acts more often than did the Indian ads in the category.

When the variable "speech acts" in advertising was analyzed within each country by type of product, the results found significant differences for several categories. Among the U.S. ads, the use of directive and poetic speech acts did not seem to vary according to durable product, non-durable product and service advertisements. The use of only "expressive speech act" was found to vary. This type of speech act was used more often by durable and service ads than non-durable product ads in the United States. Among the Indian ads, the results showed statistical significance for all three categories. Service advertisements were likely to emphasize more on expressive and directive speech acts than durable and non-durable product advertisements. On the other hand, poetic speech acts were emphasized more by durable product ads.

The analysis of the variable "comparative approach" revealed that there were some differences in the use of comparative approaches in advertisements of the two countries. The results indicated that a greater percentages of the U.S. advertisements utilized explicit and implicit comparative approaches while a greater percentage of the Indian ads used unsubstantiated claims. However, the differences could not be tested for statistical significance with chi-square tests because of small size of cells.

The analysis of the variable "iconic image of human character" revealed that there were significant differences in advertisements of the two countries. The results revealed that the U.S. ads were more likely to use an individualistic stance, and Indian ads tended to favor a collective stance for human characters. The two countries also differed in the use of individualistic and collective stance across different product categories. The analysis revealed that the tendency that was found for the use of the individualistic and collective stance between the two countries (regardless of type of product) also held across durable product, non-durable product and service ads. These results support the notion that the degree of individualism and collectivism in different cultures (India being highly collectivist and U.S. being highly individualistic) are reflected in the use of the visual stance of human characters. These findings are in agreement with those of other researchers (e.g., Alden et al., 1993; Frith & Wesson, 1991) which indicated that advertising in highly individualistic cultures uses the individualistic visual stance more often and advertising in highly collectivist cultures tends to use the collective visual stance more frequently. When the variable "iconic image of human character" in advertising was analyzed within each country by type of product, the results indicated that the use of the individualistic and collective stance did not vary within each individual country across product categories, thus supporting the contention that the significant differences that were found between the two countries would hold regardless of product type.

The analysis of the variable "indexical feature transfer" revealed that the ads of the two countries were similar in the use of physical attractiveness attribute, status attribute and loving-caring attribute. The two countries also exhibited similarities in the use of indexical feature transfer in advertising across different types of product. When the variable indexical feature transfer in advertising was analyzed within each country by type of product, the results indicated that the use of the three indexical feature transfer techniques did not vary across the three product categories.

The analysis of the variable "iconic image of women" revealed that there were significant differences in the way advertisements of the two countries portrayed women. The results indicated that a greater percentage of the Indian ads contained stereotypical images of women. On the other hand, a greater percentage of the U.S. ads used physical exploitation of women and portrayed women as sex objects. These results support the notion that differences in cultures of the two countries (India being comparatively more socially conservative with "high power distance" and U.S. being comparatively more socially liberal with "low power distance") are reflected in the portrayal of women in advertising. These findings are in agreement with those of other researchers (e.g., Alden et al., 1993) which indicated that advertising in more traditional and socially conservative cultures contains more stereotypical images of women.

The two countries also differed in the portrayal of women across several product categories. The results revealed that the tendency that was found for the stereotypical portrayal of women between the two countries (regardless of type of product) also held across durable and non-durable product ads. The tendency that was found for the physical exploitation of women between the two countries (regardless of type of product) also held across service ads. When the variable iconic image of women in advertising was analyzed within each country by type of product, the results did not find any differences which were statistically significant, thus supporting the contention that the significant differences that were found between the two countries would hold regardless of product type if differences were also found between countries across different product categories.

104

Analyses of several demographic variables found significant differences between the two countries in the use of male and female characters in advertising. The results indicated that a greater percentage of the U.S. ads featured male characters alone. This tendency also held across product type between the two countries. When the demographic variables were analyzed within each country by type of product, the results showed no statistically significant differences, thus supporting the contention that the significant differences that were found between the two countries would hold regardless of product type.

Among the similarities between the two countries were the use of elderly, children, cartoons and animals in advertising. This tendency also held across durable product and service advertisements between the two countries for all four variables. The only difference found was for the use of elderly in non-durable product ads. The results revealed that the U.S. ads used elderly characters more often than did the Indian ads. When the demographic variables were analyzed within each country by type of product, the results showed no statistically significant differences.

An analysis of each variable by type of magazine within each individual country did not show significant differences for any variable, and therefore, no comparisons were made between countries by type of magazine.

In conclusion, the findings of this study revealed that there were significant differences in the way the two cultures produced advertising messages and that differential cultural values were reflected in their advertising expressions. The evidence of specific cross-cultural differences suggests that perhaps the proponents of "standardization of international advertising" have promoted an oversimplification. This cross-cultural study adds to recent empirical evidence that suggests that despite some convergence of values, norms and lifestyles in some segments of affluent consumers in many countries, there are still numerous points on which diverse cultures of the world differ. Therefore, caution should be exercised when considering standardization in advertising and other forms of promotional communication between divergent cultures.

105

From a pragmatic standpoint, the findings of this study provide useful insights into the nature of advertising in India and the United States in the 1990s. The results show what elements and aspects of advertising are different or similar between the two cultures. From the standpoint of international promotional communication, such cross-cultural understanding is imperative in order to be able to formulate effective localized advertising or public relations messages that would appeal to or reflect the cultural values and norms of its intended audience. In a broader sense, a localized approach is beneficial not only to international communicators (more effective in getting their messages across) but also to the larger host society (its culture is not adversely affected by alien values and beliefs). The findings of this study are especially relevant and timely in light of the fact that in the 1990s, Western and Eastern cultures have come into greater contact due to a significant increase in international trade. This increased contact between the West and the East has created a need for a better understanding of international promotional communication.

From a sociological standpoint, the analysis of the variable "portrayals of women" provides useful insights into how gender role norms are manifest in advertising of the two cultures. Despite the differences in the level of portrayals, it is evident that advertising of both cultures still portray women stereotypical roles. Although considerable changes have taken place within both cultures in terms of gender roles following the women's liberation movement, the images of women in advertising are not keeping pace with the social change. Comparatively, the Indian advertisements are more stereotypical than their U.S. counterparts. This can be attributed to the fact that the women's liberation movement was slow to develop in India. This is also partly due to the fact that Indian culture is "high on power distance" meaning that power is more unequally distributed, the roles of men and women are more clearly distinguished and the pressure to maintain these distinctions is quite strong. On the other hand, because of a more traditional orientation in society, advertising in India does not use sexual portrayals of women as much as does U.S. advertising. When the findings of this study were compared with those of previous studies of U.S. advertisements in the 1970s and 1980s, it was evident that although U.S.

advertising still portrays women in stereotypical roles and as sex objects, the degree of traditional and sexual portrayals has decreased in the 1990s. The stereotypical portrayal is down from 50 to 70 percent in the 1980s to about 33 percent in the 1990s. The sexual portrayal is down from 50 to 55 percent in the 1980s to about 26 percent (moderate to high exploitation). The use of female characters alone is up from 10 to 12 percent in the 1980s to about 25 percent in the 1990s. There was no previous study of Indian advertising that could be compared with the findings of the present study.

This study examined how promotional communication expressions differ as a result of cultural differences across three product categories and two magazine categories in India and the United States. There is certainly a need to widen the research ground covered in this study. Future studies might focus on promotional communications in other types of publications and the electronic media (e.g., television). In addition to the dimensions examined in this study, there are many other variables that should be investigated. This study's comparison between developed and developing countries should also be extended to include newly industrialized countries. Additional insights and information generated by more cross-cultural research would be especially valuable in light of increased international trade and the subsequent need to communicate effectively to people of diverse cultures.

REFERENCES

Alden, D.L., Hoyer, W.D. & Lee, C. (1993, April). Identifying global and culture specific dimensions of humor in advertising: A multidimensional analysis. *Journal of Marketing, 57,* 54-75.

Anderson, R. & Engledow, J. (1977). A factor analytic comparison of U.S. and German information seekers. *Journal of Consumer Research , 3,* 185-196.

Arlett, D. (1988, April 4). Fish and tips [Debate on differences in creative standards of U.S. and U.K.]. *Advertising Age,* pp. 28-29.

Barthes, R. (1964, 1977). *Image--Music--Text.* NY: Hill & Wang.

Belch, G. E. & Belch, M.A. (1990). *Introduction to advertising and promotion management.* Chicago: Irwin.

Bellah, R.N. (1987). Habits of the hearts: *Individualism and commitment in American life.* Beverley, CA: University of California Press.

Belk, R.W. & Pollay, R.W. (March 1985). Images of ourselves: The good life in twentieth century advertising. *Journal of Consumer Research, 11,* 887-897.

Belk, R.W. & Bryce, W.J. (1986). Materialism and individual determinism in U.S. and Japanese television advertising. In Richard J. Lutz (ed.), *Advances in consumer research* (pp. 568-572). Boston: Kent.

Beniger, J.R. & Westney, D.E. (1981). Japanese and U.S. media: Graphics as a reflection of newspapers' social role. *Journal of Communication, 31* (4), 28-36.

Berger, P.L. & Kellner, H. (1981). *Sociology reinterpreted.* NY: Doubleday.

Berman, R. (1981). *Advertising and social change.* Newbury Park, CA: Sage.

Biswas, A., Olsen, J.E. & Carlet, V. (1992). A comparison of print advertisements from the U.S. and France. *Journal of Advertising, 21* (4), 73-82.

Boddewyn, J.J., Soehl, R. & Picard, T. (1986, November 29). Standardization in international marketing: Is Ted Levitt in fact right? *Business Horizons,* pp. 69-75.

Boote, A.S. (1983). Psychological segmentation in Europe. *Journal of Advertising Research, 22* (6), 19-25.

Bowen, L. & Chaffee, S.H. (1974). Product involvement and pertinent advertising appeals. *Journalism Quarterly, 51*.

Britt, S.H. (1974). Standardizing marketing for the international market. *Columbia Journal of World Business, 9* (4), 39-45.

Burli-Storz, C. (1980). *Deliberate Ambiguity in Advertising*. Geneva, Switzerland: Francke Verlag Bern.

Buzzell, R.D. (1968). Can you standardize multinational marketing? *Harvard Business Review, 46*, 102-113.

Caffyn, J. & Rogers, N. (1970). British reactions to tv commercials. *Journal of Advertising Research, 10*, 21-27.

Campbell, N.C., Graham, J.L., Jolibert, A. & Meissner, H.G. (1988). Marketing negotiations in France, Germany, U.K. and United States. *Journal of Marketing, 52*, 49 62.

Carey, J.W. (1973). Communication and culture. In C. Geertz (Ed.), *Interpretation of Cultures*. New York: Basic Books.

Carson, D. (1967). *International marketing: A comparative approach*. New York: Wiley.

Cateora, P. (1987). *International marketing*. Chicago: Irwin.

Chase, D. (1984, June 25). Agencies wrangle in world brand race. *Advertising Age*, pp. 49, 73.

Chase, D. (1984, March 19). World brand trend grows. *Advertising age*.

Clancy, K.J. (1990). The coming revolution in advertising: Ten developments which will separate winners from losers. *Journal of Advertising Research, 30*, 47-52.

Cole, S. (1980). *The sociological method*. New York: Houghton Mifflin.

Colvin, M., Heeler, R. & Thorpe, J. (1980). Developing international advertising strategy. *Journal of Marketing, 44*, 73-79.

Coser, L.A., Nock, S.L., Steffan, P.A. & Rhea, B. (1987). *Introduction to sociology*. New York: Harcourt Brace Jovanovich.

Courtney, A.E. & Lockeretz, S.W. (1971, February). A women's place: An analysis of the roles portrayed by women in magazine advertisements. *Journal of Marketing Research, 8*, 92-95.

Courtney, A.E. & Whipple, T.W. (1974). Women in TV commercials. *Journal of Communication, 24*, 110-118.

Courtney, A.E. & Whipple, T.W. (1983). *Sex Stereotyping in Advertising*. Boston: Lexington Books

Cundiff, E.W. & Hilger, M.T. (1984). *Marketing in the international environment* (pp. 322-344). Englewood Cliffs, NJ: Prentice-Hall.

Cutler, B. D. & Jivalgi, R.D. (1992). A cross-cultural analysis of the visual components of print advertising: The United States and the European Community. *Journal of Advertising Research, 32* (1), 71-80.

Diamond, R.S. (1969, August 15). Managers away from home. *Fortune*, p. 56.

Dichter, E. (1962). The world customer. *Harvard Business Review, 40*, 113-122.

Donnelly, J.H., Jr., & Ryans, J.K. (1969). Standardized global advertising: A call as yet unanswered. *Journal of Marketing, 33*, 57-60.

Donnelly, J.H., Jr. (1970). Attitudes toward culture and approach to international advertising. *Journal of Marketing, 34*, 60-68.

Dowling, G. (1980). Information content in U.S. and Australian television advertising. *Journal of Marketing, 44*, 34-37.

Dunn, S.W. (1966). The case study approach in cross national research. *Journal of Marketing Research, 3*, 26-31.

Dunn, S.W. (1974). The changing legal climate for marketing and advertising in Europe. *Columbia Journal of World Business, 9* (2), 91-98.

Dunn, S.W. & Yorke, D. (1974). European executives look at advertising. *Columbia Journal of World Business, 9* (4), 26-32.

Dunn, S.W. (1976). Effect of national identity of multinational promotional strategy in Europe. *Journal of Marketing, 40,* 50-5.

Dyer, G. (1982). *Advertising as Communication.* London: Metheun.

Eco, U. (1977, 1979). *A theory of semiotics.* Bloomington: Indiana University Press.

Elinder, E. (1965). How international can European advertising be? *Journal of Marketing, 29,* 7-11.

Ewen, S. & Ewen, E. (1982). *Channels of desire: Mass images and the shaping of American consciousness.* New York: McGraw-Hill.

Fatt, A.C. (1967). The danger of "local" international advertising. *Journal of Marketing, 31* (1), 60-62.

Fejes, F. (1980). The growth of multinational advertising agencies in Latin America. *Journal of Communication, 30* (4), 36-48.

Ferguson, J. H., Kreshel, P. J. & Tinkham, S. F. (1990). In the pages of Ms.: Sex role portrayals of women in advertising. *Journal of Advertising, 19* (1), 40-51.

Fiske, J. (1987). *Television Culture.* London: Methuen.

Fiske, J. & Hartley, J. (1978, 1980). *Reading Television. London:* Mathuen.

Frazer, C.F. (1983). Creative strategy: A management perspective. *Journal of Advertising, 12,* 36-41.

Friedmann, R. (1986). Psychological meaning of products: A simplification of the standardization vs. adaptation debate. *Columbia Journal of World Business, 21,* 97-104.

Frith, K.T. & Wesson, D. (1991, Spring-Summer). A comparison of cultural values in British and American print advertising: A study of magazine. *Journalism Quarterly, 68* (1-2), 216-224.

Fujitake, K. (1990). The transition and future of marketing research: A changing industrial and social structure. *Journal of Advertising Research, 30,* 58-67.

Gagnard, A. & Swartz, J.E. (1988). Top American advertising managers view agencies and research. *Journal of Advertising Research, 28,* 35-40.

Gilly, M.C. (1988). Sex roles in advertising. *Journal of Marketing, 52* (2), 75-85.

Graham, J.L., Kamins, M.A. & Oetomo, D.S. (1993, June). Content analysis of German and Japanese advertising in print media. *Journal of Advertising, 22* (2), 5-15.

Green, R.T., & Langeard, E. (1975). A cross national comparison of consumer habits and innovator characteristics. *Journal of Marketing, 39,* 34-41.

Green, R.T., Cunningham, W.H. & Cunningham, I.M. (1975). The effectiveness of standardized global advertising. *Journal of Advertising, 4* (3), 25-30.

Hall, E.T. (1976). *Beyond Culture.* New York: Anchor Books.

Hall, E.T. & Hall, M.R. (1990). *Understanding Cultural Differences: Germans, French and Americans.* Yarmouth, ME: Intercultural Press.

Harmon, R.R., Razzouk, N.Y. & Stern, B. L. (1983). The information content of comparative magazine advertisements. *Journal of Advertising, 12* (4), 10-19.

Haskins, J. & Kendrick, A. (1991). *Successful advertising research methods.* Chicago: NTC Business Books.

Hawkins, D.I. & Kenneth, A.C. (1976). Advertising and differentiated sex roles in contemporary American society. *Journal of the Academy of Marketing Science, 4,* 418-428.

Henry, W.A. (1976). Cultural values do correlate with consumer behavior. *Journal of Marketing Research, 13,* 121-127.

Hite, R.E. & Fraser, C. (1988). International advertising strategies of multinational corporations. *Journal of Advertising Research, 28,* 9-17.

Hofstede, G. (1983). National cultures in four dimensions. *International Studies of Management and Organization, 13* (2), 52-63.

Holbrook, M. B. (July, 1987). Mirror, mirror, on the wall, what's unfair in the reflections on advertising. *Journal of Marketing, 51,* 95-103.

Holsti, O. (1969). *Content analysis for the social sciences and humanities.* Boston: Addison-Wesley.

Hong, J.W., Muderrisoglu, A. & Zinkhan, G.M. (1987). Cultural differences and advertising expression: A comparative content analysis of U.S. and Japanese magazine advertising. *Journal of Advertising, 16* (1), 55-62.

Hornik, J. (1980). Comparative evaluation of international vs. national advertising strategies. *Columbia Journal of World Business, 15,* 36-46.

Hornik, J. & Rubinow, S. (1981). Expert respondents synthesis for international advertising research. *Journal of Advertising Research, 1* (3), 9-16.

Howitt, D. (1982). *The Mass Media and Social Problems (International series in social psychology.* Oxford: Pergamon Press.

Hsia, H.J. (1988). *Mass Communications Research Methods.* Hilisdale, NJ: Erlbaum.

Ishida, E. (1974). *Japanese culture: A study of origins and characteristics.* (Teruko Kachi, Trans.). Honolulu: University of Hawaii Press.

Kahle, L.R. (1988). Changes in social values in the U.S. during the past decade. *Journal of Advertising Research, 28,* 35-41.

Kaynak, E. & Mitchell, L.A. (1981). Analysis of marketing strategies used in diverse cultures. *Journal of Advertising Research, 21* (3), 25-32.

Klassen, M.L., Jasper, C.R. & Schwartz, A. M. (1993). Men and women: Images of their relationships in magazine advertisements. *Journal of Advertising Research,* 30-39.

Kotler, P. (1983). *Principles of marketing.* Englewood Cliffs, NJ: Prentice-Hall.

Kotler, P. (1986). Global standardiztion--courting danger. *Journal of Consumer Marketing, 3,* 13-15.

Krippendorf, K. (1980). *Content analysis: An introduction to its methodology.* Newbury Park, CA: Sage.

Lannon, J. (1986). New techniques for understanding consumer reactions to advertising. *Journal of Advertising Research, 26* (4), RC6-9.

Leech, G.N. (1966). *English in advertising*. London: Longman.

Leiss, W., Kline, S. & Jhally, S. (1986). *Social Communication in Advertising*. New York: Metheun.

Levitt, T. (1983). The globalization of markets. *Harvard Business Review, 61*(3), 92-102.

Light, L. (1990). The changing advertising world. *Journal of Advertising Research, 30,* 30-35.

Lipset, S. M. (1963). *The first new nation: The United States in historical and comparative perspective.* New York: Basic Books.

Lorimor, E.S. & Dunn, S.W. (1967). Four measures of cross cultural advertising effectiveness. *Journal of Advertising Research, 7,* 10-13.

Lysonski, S. (1983, Summer). Female and male portrayals in magazine advertisements: A re-examination. *Akron Business Review, 14,* 45-50.

Madden, C., Caballero, M., & Matsukubo, S. (1986). An analysis of information content in U.S. and Japanese magazine advertising. *Journal of Advertising, 15* (3), 38-45.

Mattelart, A. (1983). *Transnationals and the third world: The struggle for culture.* Boston: Bergin and Garvey.

McCracken, G. (1986, June). Culture and consumption: A theoretical account of the structure and movement of the cultural meanings of consumer goods. *Journal of Consumer Research, 13,* 71-84.

McDaniel, C., Jr. (1982). *Marketing*. New York: Harper & Row.

McQuail, D. (1994). *Mass communication theory: An introduction*. London: Sage.

Monette, D.R., Sullivan, T.J. & Dejong, C.R. (1986). *Applied Social Research*. New York: Holt, Rinehart and Winston.

Mooij, M.K., & Keegan, W. J. (1991). *Advertising worldwide*. Englewood Cliffs, NJ: Prentice-Hall.

Moriarity, S.E. (1989). A content analysis of visuals used in print media advertising. *Journalism Quarterly, 66* (1), 550-554.

Mueller, B. (1987). An analysis of information content in standardized vs. specialized multinational advertisements. *Journal of International Business Studies, 23-39.*

Mueller, B. (1987). Reflections of culture: An analysis of Japanese and American advertising appeals. *Journal of Advertising Research, 27,* 51-59.

Munson, J.M. & McIntyre, S.H. (1979, February). Developing practical procedures for the measurement of personal values in cross-cultural marketing. *Journal of Marketing Research, 16,* 48-52.

Navarro, M. (1979). Research on Latin American women. Signs: *Journal of Women in Culture and Society, 5* (11), 111-120.

Nishikawa, T. (1990). New product development: Japanese consumer tastes in the area of electronics and home appliance. *Journal of Advertising Research, 30,* 27-30.

Nishina, S. (1990). Japanese consumers: Introducing foreign products/brands into the Japanese market. *Journal of Advertising Research, 30,* 35-45.

Noth, W. (1990). *Handbook of Semiotics.* Bloomington: Indiana University Press.

Noth, W. (1988). The language of commodities. *International Journal of Research in Marketing, 4,* 173-186.

O'Connor, J. (1974). International advertising. *Journal of Advertising, 3,* 9-14.

Okechuku, C. & Wang, G. (1988). The effectiveness of Chinese print ad in North America. *Journal of Advertising Research, 28,* 25-26.

Olson, J.L. (1977). Women and social change in a Mexican town. *Journal of Anthropological Research, 33,* 73-88.

Onkvisit, S. & Shaw, J.J. (1983). Identifying marketing attributes necessary for standardized international advertising. *Mid-Atlantic Journal of Business, 22,* 43-57.

Onkvisit, S. & Shaw, J.J. (1985). A view of marketing and advertising practices in Asia and its meaning for marketing managers. *Journal of Consumer Marketing, 2* (1), 5-17.

Onkvisit, S. & Shaw, J.J. (1987). Standardized international advertising. *Columbia Journal of World Business, 25,* 43-55.

Ortner, S.B. (1974). Is female to male as nature is to culture? In Rosaldo, M.Z. & Lamphere, L. (eds), *Women, Culture and Society*, San Francisco, CA: Stanford University Press.

Poe, A. (1976). Active women in ads. *Journal of Communication, 26*, 185-192.

Pollay, R.W. (1986). The distorted mirror: Reflections on the unintended consequences of advertising. *Journal of Marketing, 50*, 18-36.

Pollay, R.W. (1987). On the value of reflections on the values in 'The distorted mirror.' *Journal of Marketing, 51*, 104-109.

Plummer, J.T. (1977). Consumer focus in cross-national research. *Journal of Advertising, 6* (2), 5-15.

Pryor, M.H. (1965). Planning in a worldwide business. *Harvard Business Review, 43* (1), 130-139.

Plutchil, R. (1980). *A psychoevolutionary synthesis*. New York: Harper & Row.

Ramaprashad, J. (1992). Informational content of American and Japanese television commercials. *Journalism Quarterly, 69* (3), 612-623.

Resnik, A. & Stern, B. (1977). An analysis of informational content in television advertising. *Journal of Marketing*, 50-53.

Ricks, D.A. (1983). *Big business blunders*. Chicago: Irwin.

Rice, M.D. & Lu, Z. (1988). A content analysis of Chinese magazine advertisements. *Journal of Advertising, 17*, 43-48.

Rokeach, M. (1973). *The Nature of Human Values*. New York: Free Press.

Rosen, B.N., Boddewyn, J.J. & Louis, E.A. (1988). Participation by U.S. agencies in international brand advertising: An empirical study. *Journal of Advertising, 17* (4), 14-22.

Rosenau, P.M. (1992). *Post-modernism and the Social Sciences*. Englewood Cliffs, NJ: Princeton University Press.

Rothenberg, R. (1989, July 2). Brits buy up the ad business. *The New York Times Magazines*. p. 14.

Ryans, J.K. (1969). Is it too soon to put a tiger in every tank? *Columbia Journal of World Business, 4,* 69-75.

Samover, L.A. & Porter, R.E. (1991). *Communication between cultures.* Belmont, CA: Wadsworth.

Schiller, H. (1983). Informatics and information flows: The underpinnings of transnational capitalism. In V. Moscow & J. Wasko (Eds.), *The Critical Communication Review* (Vol. 2, pp. 3-29). Englewood Cliffs, NJ: Ablex.

Schleifer, S. & Dunn, S.W. (1968). Relative effectiveness of advertisements of foreign and domestic origin. *Journal of Marketing Research, 5,* 296-298.

Schmalensee, D.H. (1983). Today's top priority advertising research questions. *Journal of Advertising Research, 23* (2), 49-60.

Schneider, K.C. & Schneider, S. B. (1979, Summer). Trends in sex roles in television commercials. *Journal of Marketing, 43,* 79-84.

Schoell, W.F. (1985). *Marketing.* Boston: Allyn & Bacon.

Schulman, R.S. (1992). *Statistics in Plain English with Computer Applications.* New York: Van Nostrand Reinhold.

Searle, J.R. (1969, 1971). *The Philosophy of Language.* London: Oxford University Press.

Scott, W.A. (1969). Reliability of content analysis. *Public Opinion Quarterly, 19,* 321-325.

Sepstrup, P. (1981). Methodological development in content analysis. In K.E. Rosengren (Ed.), *Advances in content analysis.* Beverly Hills, CA: Sage.

Shaw, J.J. & Onkvisit, S. (1983). Letters to the editor. *Journal of Advertising Research, 23* (6), 60-61.

Shiffman, L.G. & Kanuk, L. (1978). *Consumer Behavior.* Englewood Cliffs, NJ: Prentice-Hall.

Silverstein, A.J. & Silverstein, R. (1974). The portrayal of women in television advertising, *Federal Communications Bar Journal, 27* (1), 71-93.

Sorenson, R.Z. & Wiechmann, U.E. (1975). How multinationals view standardization. *Harvard Business Review , 53,* 38.

Spatz, C & Johnston, J.O. (1984). Basic Statistics. Belmont, CA: Brooks/Cole. Stempel, III,

    G.H. (1989). Research methods in mass communication. In G.S. Stempel & B.H.

    Westley (Eds.). Content analysis. Englewood Cliffs, NJ: Prentice-Hall.

Stern, B., Resnik, A. & Krugman, D. (1981). Magazine advertising: An analysis of its

    information content. Journal of Advertising Research, 21 (2), 39-44.

Stewart, D.W. & McAuliffe, K.J. (1988). Determinants of international media purchasing: A

    survey of media buyers. Journal of Advertising, 17 (3), 22-26.

Stewart, D. & Furse, D. (1986). Effective television advertising. Boston: Lexington Books.

Tal, E. (1974). Advertising in developing countries. Journal of Advertising, 3 (2), 19-23.

Tan, A.S. (1986). Mass communication theories and research. New York: Macmillan.

Tansey, R., Hyman, M.R. & Zinkhan, G.M. (1990). Cultural themes in Brazilian and U.S. auto

    ads: A cross-cultural comparison. Journal of Advertising, 19 (2), 30-39.

Umiker-Sebeok, J. Ed. (1987). Marketing and semiotics: New directions in the study of signs for

    sale. Berlin: Mouton de Gruyter.

Vestergaard, T. & Kim, S. (1985). The Language of Advertising. New York: Blackwell.

Unwin, J.F. (1974). How culture affects advertising expression and communication style.

    Journal of Advertising, 3 (2), 24-27.

Vinson, D.E., Scott, J.E. & Lamont, L.M. (1977). The role of personal values in marketing and

    consumer behavior. Journal of Marketing, 41, 44-50.

Weichmann, U.S. (1974). Integrating multinational marketing activities. Columbia Journal of

    World Business, 9 (4), 17-23.

Weinberger, M.G. & Spotts, H.E. (1989). A situational view of information content in television

    advertising in U.S. and U.K. Journal of Marketing, 53 (1), 89-95.

Wiles, C.R. (1991). A comparison of role portrayal of men and women in magazine advertising

    in the USA and Sweden. International Journal of Advertising, 10 (3), 259-268.

Williamson, J. (1978). Decoding Advertisements. London: Marion Boyars.